SCHOOLS COUNCIL EXAMINATIONS BULLETIN 41

Review of graded tests

ANDREW HARRISON

Methuen Educational

First published 1982 for the Schools Council
160 Great Portland Street, London W1N 6LL
by Methuen Educational
11 New Fetter Lane, London EC4P 4EE

Filmset by
Northumberland Press Ltd
Gateshead, Tyne and Wear
Printed in Great Britain by
Richard Clay (The Chaucer Press) Ltd
Bungay, Suffolk

British Library Cataloguing in Publication Data

Harrison, Andrew
   Review of graded tests.—(Schools Council
examination bulletin 41)
1. Examinations—Great Britain
I. Title   II. Series
371.2′6013   LB3056.G7

ISBN 0–423–51040–1

Contents

Foreword

In 1980 the Schools Council launched five programmes of work to be undertaken over three years. Programme 5 – Improving the Examinations System – covers a large number of activities related to assessment, examinations and the recording of results, including monitoring and co-ordination of existing examinations; research into any reform which is believed to be desirable; review and evaluation of current practice and of new developments in assessment; and dissemination of information.

The present review of developments in graded tests was undertaken as part of this programme. The aim was to collate and disseminate information on the scope and nature of the widespread activity in recent years in developing graded objectives, syllabuses and tests, mostly, but not exclusively, in modern languages. The special emphasis placed by the programme on new developments in assessment and the recording of results is reflected in the special attention paid by this review to the nature and structure of the tests themselves and their relationship to work on criterion-referenced grading in public examinations.

A previous involvement of the Council in the field of graded tests concentrated on evaluating the effects of these tests on the attitudes of pupils, teachers and parents to the learning of French. That Council-sponsored project studied the North Yorkshire/Leeds scheme and resulted in a report by M. Buckby *et al.*, *Graded Objectives and Tests for Modern Languages: an Evaluation*, which was published in 1981.

The present review was conducted by Mr Andrew Harrison, to whom the Council is grateful for a thorough investigation and its clear presentation in this report. Like all other Programme 5 projects, this project was overseen by the Monitoring and Review Group (a list of whose members is presented on p. 83) set up for this purpose by the Council's Examinations Committee.

LEA ORR
Principal Research Officer
Schools Council

7

Acknowledgements

I am grateful to GOML groups for their help and interest, both those who responded so positively to the questionnaire and particularly those who welcomed me on self-invited visits; to the examination boards for answering my enquiries and especially to their research staffs for essential discussions about principles; to many other correspondents for the information they provided, even when it was negative; and finally to the Steering Group – Lea Orr, Peter Dines, Lesley Kant and Geoff Bardell – who guided the project and established the shape of the report.

ANDREW HARRISON

8

I. Introduction

Over the past five years or so groups of teachers in Britain have been developing new teaching and assessment materials for school pupils in modern languages, mainly in French and German. These developments have brought fresh motivation to pupils and have encouraged teachers to discuss and rethink their objectives. There were in May 1981 about fifty-eight groups working on schemes of Graded Objectives in Modern Languages (GOML), but even though they were all based on similar aims and had many methodological principles in common, they were autonomous and regarded themselves as independent local schemes. The movement, if so it can be called, is a comparatively rare phenomenon: a nationwide pattern of individual groups within which teachers work together to try to solve common problems in a particular field. This individual impetus of the groups makes GOML developments remarkable even in Britain, where it is taken for granted that there exists some independence and autonomy for each school within the overall system.

A conference was organized by CILT (the Centre for Information on Language Teaching and Research) in April 1979 to take stock of the bases on which schemes were being constructed and give an opportunity to the groups to institute a framework for mutual information and consultation. It was attended by representatives of the forty or so groups then existing and others with interest and technical expertise in the various fields concerned (for example linguistics, psychology, education, psychometrics and educational administration). As a result of this meeting a GOML Coordinating Committee was set up which has issued a series of newsletters and organized conferences for GOML representatives, with the help of funding from CILT. In addition, groups have been requested to send in information to the CILT library, which holds a series of continually updated files giving details of schemes throughout Great Britain.

An educational development of this size clearly has wide implications not only for the subject involved, in this case modern languages, but also for other subjects. In addition, since a major part of the success of GOML systems relates to short-term goals marked by achievement tests and certificates, there may be implications for assessment in general, especially in relation to proposals for a new examination system at 16+.

The present investigation was therefore set up to find out about:

> the scope, practice, essential features and implications of graded test systems;
> the methods used in graded test schemes in grading and recording attainment;
> the relationship of graded test schemes to public examinations;
> possible implications for other areas of the curriculum.

These aims relate specifically to tests, not to teaching, but the separation of teaching from testing is impracticable, and the report refers continually to the content of courses.

The idea of graded tests does not originate with GOML groups, and reference has been made from the beginning[1] to grades I to VIII of the Associated Board of the Royal Schools of Music, which has been conducting local examinations in music since 1889. Other parallels have been drawn with sport certificates[2] (Amateur Swimming Association, founded 1869) and awards for achievement[3] (Boy Scouts, established 1908, Duke of Edinburgh's Award from 1956). There have been precedents too in language examinations, such as those set by the Institute of Linguists[4] (founded 1910) and the English Speaking Board[5] (founded 1953). Developments in other secondary-school subjects include the Kent Mathematics Project[6] (1967 onwards) and investigations of progressive assessments in science[7] (1972 onwards). The difficulty in considering all these possible examples of 'graded tests' is deciding what defines the concept for the purposes of this investigation. If the common ground of GOML groups is taken as a model, it may well appear that there is no other scheme quite like them; on the other hand, a wide definition would include GCE examinations, which are graded (but in a different sense) within ordinary level and advanced level, and are in many subjects progressive from one level to the other, even though the examinations they provide are in their present form considered by GOML to be contrary in both principle and practice to the aims of GOML groups.

Some account of the background to graded tests in the various areas needs to be given before a definition of the term can be attempted. It is convenient, if arbitrary, to discuss these areas under five headings: language examinations; the performing arts; sport; technical skills; and classroom subjects.

10

The following account of the origins and ethos of GOML groups in general (from Harding, Page and Rowell, *Graded Objectives in Modern Languages*) is worth quoting at length because it suggests a basis for setting up a working hypothesis for criteria by which a graded test system can be recognized.

The basic principles of the Graded Objectives Scheme for Modern Language Learning, as they are at present realized, were first expressed in opposition to the plans for new public examinations to be taken at age sixteen-plus ... The proposed sixteen-plus examination ... took for granted the principle of the five-year course which must be completed before a public examination could be taken. But a five-year course is irrelevant to most language learners in the new secondary schools. It is wasteful and illogical to start pupils off on a course which two thirds of them will not complete ... It is necessary to propose goals which more pupils can reach and by doing so experience success in language learning. The first principle of the graded objectives scheme was therefore that the traditional five-year course to CSE O level should be broken up into a set of shorter-term objectives, each one leading to the next and each one building directly on its predecessor ...

The most worthwhile objectives would seem to be the ability to use the language for realistic purposes rather than, for example, the ability to describe the language or use it for purposes which the actual user would rarely need to employ. The second principle of the graded examinations scheme was therefore that objectives should be behavioural, that is, they should be defined in terms of what tasks a candidate would be able to perform in the language ... It was clear that communicative competence in practical situations ... was a skill needed by all language learners and not simply by those who would opt out after two or three years. The graded objectives therefore would not be tied to an ability range: they would not be specifically aimed at low-ability learners. They would represent steps in a continuum which could be attempted by all learners ... It followed then that the objectives should not be tied to an age range either, so that anyone, in school or out, of any age, would be able to attempt any level of which she might think herself capable. Thus the third principle was established: that the graded objectives would not be aimed at a particular age or level of ability but would be available to both adults and school pupils irrespective of their perceived ability ...

The model itself proceeds from the conviction that a high percentage of all learners should be able to attain some measurable standard of achievement in a modern language. This achievement should be seen as the successful completion of a series of closely defined tasks in communicative situations. Analogies may be drawn with sport or music examinations or even the driving test ... Ideally the tests may be taken at any time when learners feel that they are ready, in much the same way as Scouts, Guides, entrants for the Duke of Edinburgh's award, etc., take their tests at times suitable to themselves. Some schemes are already experimenting with this approach, but since this implies obvious organizational problems in school, it may never be possible to have the tests 'on offer' in the way originally intended.[8]

The other organizations providing language examinations in a series of grades or stages are the Institute of Linguists and the English Speaking Board, the former regarding them as steps towards professional qualifications in translating and interpreting and the latter as stages in the encouragement of a vital developmental skill for all speakers of English. Examinations in languages are also set as complementary to commercial subjects and in spoken English as ancillaries to music and to speech and drama.

In the performing arts themselves, which include for present purposes music, speech and drama, and dance, the syllabuses and examinations have various origins. Some have arisen from a desire to improve standards of education in the subject, some have been developed in relation to existing courses at teaching institutions, and others have come into existence as a service for teachers and a promotion of the commercial interests of private schools and teachers of the subject. But it is likely that there are elements of these three aims in the production of all examinations in this area, though the emphasis placed on each aim varies with the organizing body. It is clear too that the natural disposition of grades – fairly close together in level at the bottom but spreading out into greater differentiation further up – is a reflection both of the educational pyramid in which many students start subjects but few reach the higher levels, and also of the economic interests of examining bodies, which need large numbers of candidates at the simpler and more easily organized lower levels in order to help finance the higher levels, which are more demanding in time and examiner expertise.

The aim of the often-quoted Amateur Swimming Association (ASA) certificates is to promote swimming as a means to accident prevention and as a recreation and a competitive sport. The first of these aims is unique to swimming as a sport: others, such as football and hockey, use schemes of graded awards to promote interest in the sport among young people ('for all children who are sufficiently interested in football to want to become better at it'; 'to encourage young players to improve ...'), but they also presumably have the last two of the ASA's aims in mind as well.

The technical skills are mainly those connected with office practice.

12

Their intention is to provide achievement certificates for those who wish to prove proficiency in various skills at various levels, as an aid to promotion at work and as an element in job satisfaction. As with the music and dance examinations, the grades or stages are usually closer together at the lower end, presumably for much the same reasons.

Tests in other classroom subjects are mainly in mathematics and science. With a few exceptions, the mathematics schemes are taken by pupils at the end of their secondary-school course, and are usually intended as certificates of basic numeracy for those pupils who are not taking either CSE or GCE, and so would not otherwise have any certificated achievement in the subject. The tests therefore represent one-off, terminal assessments, and are not graded in the sense of either music examinations or GOML tests. The exceptions are tests which are set and taken as integral parts of courses, and the intention here is both motivating and diagnostic, since both pupil and teacher can see a direct relationship between the course and the test result. The origin of the assessments in science referred to above is a research project which investigated the relationship between cognitive development and the demands of the curriculum and established that there is a mismatch which is now the subject of further research. The tests in this project are therefore related not to an abstract series of grades but to empirically determined levels of pupil development.

It appears from the above discussion that the GOML schemes represent a much more restricted view of the concept 'graded test' than other schemes or patterns of examination with which they have been compared. The essence of the GOML quotation given above is that a graded test scheme is progressive, with short-term objectives leading on from one to the next; that it is task-oriented, relating to the use of language for practical purposes; and that it is closely linked into the learning process, with pupils or students taking the tests when they are ready to pass. The only elements which are common to all the examinations so far mentioned in this report are progression, since they all incorporate a series of tests at increasing levels of difficulty, and motivation, which is common to all examinations in the sense that they set a goal to be reached, but which is only part of the contribution which GOML tests intend to make to learning. Some of the tests (particularly in sport) are set in the form of tasks to be completed, but this does not necessarily run in parallel with the approach through behavioural objectives which has been adopted by GOML groups.

Some framework, however, had to be set up which would give coherence

13

to the report, and it seemed logical, if the existence and success of GOML groups were the starting point for the investigation, to take their principles as a guide for enquiry.

Some information about GOML groups was already available, particularly in Harding *et al.* (1980), the files at CILT and the newsletters produced by the GOML Coordinating Committee. A Schools Council evaluation of one of the GOML schemes had also reported on many of the benefits of adopting the new approach.[9] In other subjects published syllabuses of examinations could be obtained. Enquiries were made by letter to subject associations, the chairmen of Schools Council subject committees, the GCE and CSE boards, and organizations and individuals known to be interested, and possibly involved, in assessment which might include some form of graded test. In addition, a questionnaire was devised in conjunction with another investigation (on oral/aural testing in GOML groups) to establish basic facts about the fifty-eight existing GOML schemes and to elicit opinions from those most directly involved. Replies were received from forty-four groups.

The information gathered from all these sources will be discussed in the next five chapters of this report to illustrate the following issues:

organization;
testing and teaching strategies;
certificates and public examinations;
characteristics of systems;
transferability.

In the final chapter an attempt will be made to assess the implications of this discussion for the future and to draw some conclusions about the value of graded test schemes in a wider educational context.

II. Organization

The earliest GOML schemes arose out of an urgent need to cope with the large increase in the number of pupils studying modern languages (mainly French) as a result of the reorganization of schools into a system of comprehensives. These pupils were largely from the lower ability ranges and the traditional courses which had been more or less successfully used for grammar-school pupils were not suitable for them. In addition, there had been a proportionate reduction in the number of pupils studying modern languages as reflected in the entry figures for public examinations. There was also, on the examinations front, considerable dissatisfaction with the results of the feasibility studies for a new 16+ examination system which were undertaken in 1971–4.

The questionnaire asked for information about dates of starting for GOML schemes, and dates of the first tests (see Appendix A, Table 1). It appears that some schemes took two years to reach the testing stage and some went from formation of group to testing in the same year. In general, however, two inferences seem clear: that it usually takes about two years from the start of a scheme to the beginning of testing, and that the boom year for the formation of groups was 1978, with the incidence of new schemes now falling off. Information was also sought about the number of pupils involved in GOML tests, and the replies show that in 1980 the total number for all languages at all levels was over 71,000, of which nearly 65,800 were for French, and that the equivalent estimated figures for 1981 were approximately 140,000 overall, including 122,000 for French (Table 2). More detailed information was also requested about the size of groups: the majority of groups for French in 1980 were catering for between 500 and 1000 or 1000–3000 candidates (seven groups for each range) and in 1981 the largest number of groups had 1000–3000 candidates (ten groups) (Tables 3 and 4). The largest groups are those in which the GOML tests have been adopted for general use in LEA areas, but even there the testing is regarded as a service to schools rather than an LEA policy. The largest group of all was expecting 12,000 candidates in 1981 for French at level 1. The smallest groups tend to be those which set a deliberate limit (say ±200) on entries by restricting the scheme

15

to a small number of schools so that teachers can continue to be directly involved in the preparation of materials and marking of tests. Advice and materials are, however, available to other groups who wish to set up separately.

The flexible application of GOML materials to different situations is also evident in the definition of levels. It was clear from the outset that level 1 was not necessarily to be equated with year 1 of the secondary-school course or level 2 with year 2, and so on up to the fifth year. On the other hand it seemed important for this review to try to find out how far the levels could be regarded as equivalent across groups. The answer is, hardly at all (Table 5). The variations are considerable, with eighteen different lengths of learning time mentioned, and the only ones to reach any size at all are one year for level 1 (mentioned eight times); two years for level 1 (eight); three years for level 2 (eleven). The question covers a more complex situation even than this, since if one of the principles of graded tests is that they can be taken by anyone on demand, when s/he is ready and likely to pass, the answer to the question as asked should be '1–5' for each of the five levels.

The use of resources is a major factor in the successful organization of any curriculum development programme (as in general terms GOML schemes are). Information was requested about financial arrangements and the answers show that for most groups, no charge is made for the tests. This seems to imply that LEAs are funding many GOML developments, but this support is by no means universal and in addition to any physical services provided by LEAs (for example paper, typing, duplicating) most schemes are founded on the willingness of teachers to spend many hours of their own time attending meetings (including in some cases long and awkward journeys) and producing materials. This hidden cost is considerable. Where a charge is made, it is usually as a fee per candidate (ranging from 20p to 50p), but these fees are normally met by the LEA, so that payment apparently amounts merely to a transfer from one account to another within the authority. Expenses for schools are more common (seventeen groups stated that there were extra costs for schools, twenty that there were not): these relate mainly to duplicating and provision of blank tapes or cassettes.

There are implications for class organization in the award or withholding of certificates. What happens to those pupils who are not awarded a certificate is not clear (Table 6). In principle, if tests are taken when pupils are ready for them, and so likely to succeed, this problem rarely arises, and it is perhaps because of this that respondents often said that there was no fixed procedure, or that procedures varied considerably within the scheme, even if a second principle which follows on from the first is that success in level 1 should lead immediately on to work towards level 2, resulting in the formation of new groups of pupils within classes.

A relatively minor organizational point, but one which relates to how far the language learnt is 'useful', and seen to be so, is the intended audience for syllabuses (Table 7). So far, they appear to be written for teachers, and less for pupil consumption than might have been expected, though two respondents did mention that an explanatory statement had been specially written for pupils.

Another organizational consideration is when in the school year the tests are available to schools. The kind of tests which are considered appropriate for any given scheme depends on the approach it takes to structuring the assessments in relation to the course. For example some schemes have test materials available at the beginning of the school year and schools ask for supplies of them (with reasonable notice) when required. This means that it is possible for pupils to take the set of tests for a given level at any time when they are ready, subject only to the organizational constraints imposed on the teacher. In practice, however, tests tend to be taken towards the end of the school year and in some schools are taken only as end-of-year examinations, by complete classes. These are examples of a single test occurring at the end of the syllabus (whether this syllabus is provided by the GOML scheme or less formally put together by the individual teacher), but there are schemes in which the certificate is awarded partly on the basis of continuous assessment, either as an element in the level test or more consciously provided for by records entered on progress (or achievement) cards for each pupil and by intermediate tests carried out with varying degrees of informality by the teacher. Here again the variety of provision is considerable.

The organization of graded test schemes in other areas is usually undertaken by examining boards set up for the purpose, either dependent on larger bodies or as autonomous entities. Exceptions are in mathematics, where the impetus has come from the very similar (though not, in this subject, new) needs of lower-ability pupils which have been answered by a wide variety of school-based schemes; and in science, where curriculum development and research have together produced the basis for assessments. The size of these schemes may be gauged from the following

17

approximate figures for 1979–80: Associated Board of the Royal Schools of Music (ABRSM): 300,000; main examining bodies for dance: 300,000 together; Football Association scheme: 50,000; Royal Society of Arts: 650,000 entries for all subjects; Duke of Edinburgh's Award: 40,000. Hertfordshire Mathematics is used in seventy-eight schools; the Kent Mathematics Project (KMP) has been used for 35,000 children over twelve years.

The problem of what the levels mean is just as difficult in other areas as it is for GOML groups, the only real difference being a longer experience. Some examination systems describe levels in terms of teaching or study hours spent (English as a foreign language – EFL), others by relating them to external reference points such as GCE (modern languages) or by average achievement for age (CSE). The understanding of what a level represents in any examination system comes with experience for those most needing to know, a rule of thumb which can amount to a consensus among groups of similarly interested parties. In general, for example, a musician will know what is meant by grade VI of the Associated Board's examinations and teachers of EFL have a fairly exact view of what the Cambridge Syndicate's First Certificate and Proficiency examinations mean in terms of level.

The cost of examinations run by boards is usually borne by the individual candidate, but within-school mathematics tests are presumably funded by the individual school (or group of schools) unless they are sponsored from the outset, or taken over, by the LEA. The sports associations are sometimes sponsored by commercial interests, which means that payment is required only for badges or certificates.

The organizational implications for candidates who are not awarded certificates obviously depend on the use made of the award. The results of the Football Association's scheme and the ASA's various schemes for swimming, for example, are certificates and badges which are valued by the recipients partly as collectors' items but more importantly as a record of achievement. Those who are not successful at the first taking simply try again later. Failure to achieve a grade certificate for violin playing or typing is more serious, partly because a higher standard of achievement is required (it is more difficult to pass and more candidates fail). In these cases, advice is often written by the examiner on a mark sheet or results slip (ABRSM, Pitman's) which is returned to the candidate to indicate where shortfall has occurred. Whether any action is taken as a result of this information is the teacher's decision, related partly to whether the

18

test is his or her own and therefore likely to have this as one of its purposes, or external, in which case remedial work is needed only for retakes.

The principle that pupils should take tests when they are ready for them (and therefore likely to succeed) is a tenet of mastery learning which applies in classroom assessments rather than external examining. Thus the grade examinations in the performing arts and technical skills are available up to three or four times a year on fixed dates. Achievement tests in the sports mentioned above are more informal, and are taken at the discretion of the instructor when the necessary equipment and facilities are available. The mathematics tests are mostly taken so as to provide school leaving certificates, but one notable exception is KMP, where the testing is an integral part of the course and leads to individualized learning. This seems to confirm that the principle of testing when the pupil is ready can be fulfilled only when the assessment is incorporated in a planned learning sequence, which is not the case in most GOML schemes.

III. Testing and teaching strategies

One of the most striking results to come from the questionnaire is how far GOML groups regard themselves as individual and autonomous. As many as 62 per cent of the French groups developed their own schemes, though five of them said they had been 'influenced by' earlier schemes, eight were adapted from other schemes and five more took over other schemes complete (Tables 8 and 9). One factor which may have encouraged the tendency to adapt schemes for local use is the question of copyright: they may have been adapted not only to make them more suitable for a particular group's pupils but also to make them legal.

It appears that in general only about half as many schemes are intended for pupils of lower ability as for all abilities, even though one of the original aims was to provide incentives for the new language learners in comprehensive schools (Tables 10, 11 and 12). In theory, 'all abilities' includes 'lower abilities', but in answer to the three questions about target groups a proportion of schemes answered that the syllabuses or tests were intended for both of these categories of learner. This seems to show again that there is variety of application within one scheme. This raises several questions of principle, such as the speed at which various groups of pupils (or indeed individuals) progress through the syllabus, the danger of schemes designed for lower-ability pupils becoming regarded as of lower value than the rest of the curriculum, and the anxiety of some teachers that programmes of work suitable for the lower-ability pupils cannot by definition provide a viable basis for more advanced work later. Another point to emerge here is the use of schemes by adults, both as learners and as testees – in fact their participation is greater so far than that of sixth-formers within the schools, which was itself a development anticipated in Harding *et al.* (1980).

The information given about syllabuses (Table 13) shows that explicit statements of syllabus content are common, and this is not very surprising because one of the fundamental principles of the graded test approach is that it provides new and helpful ways of specifying exactly what will be taught and tested. But more than half the respondents report that the syllabus is the group's own, reinforcing earlier answers

20

in which the origin of the tests was regarded as local.

The method of defining syllabuses is a difficult area of enquiry. Without extravagantly long explanations of what precisely various approaches mean, there is a considerable problem in producing a coherent description of specifications in general. The simplest, though superficial, solution is to summarize in single words representing various current approaches to syllabus specification. This was the solution adopted for the questionnaire (Table 14). The terms used were 'structural' (a concern with grammatical forms); 'functional' (referring to the uses to which the language learnt is to be put); 'notional' (relating the content of the syllabus to the ideas and concepts which are to be expressed in the language); 'situational' (referring to the circumstances in which the language is to be used); 'lexical' (a concern with meaning); and 'the four skills' (listening, reading, speaking, writing).

The term 'situational' is most frequently indicated, perhaps because this term can be taken to describe the whole range of language material for practical applications, without commitment to any particular method for teaching it. The terms 'functional' and 'notional' have come to represent the new perspective on language learning which starts from the question: 'What will the learner want to understand and express in language?' rather than 'How much of the language does the learner have to know?' which relates to a structural approach (now, for some, outmoded) and to a lesser extent a lexical one (though the present emphasis on meaning rather than grammatical form might also incline respondents to specify 'lexical').

The content of the tests was also explored by the questionnaire (Tables 15 and 16). Here again, definition presented problems, though examples were given for titles ('e.g. speaking, listening, comprehension'). The connotation of terms may vary as in the descriptions of syllabuses, but more important, a question of principle is again involved. If the test syllabus is set up as a description of language activities related to use in real-life contexts (which is the foundation stone for the whole edifice: Harding et al., 1980), the test components might be expected to reflect this so that the assessment is of communication as it happens rather than of the individual elements which together produce it. This implies that components should be labelled not with skills but with activities. The titles given by respondents to the components of the tests (Table 15) show that most of them are labelled as skills, with six designated as mixed skills; another six titles can be classified as activities, and the final group of seven titles or comments have been listed in the table as unclassified. Five groups

21

said they could give no answer because they did not regard the test as separable into components, whether skills or anything else, and one gave no weightings. One group denied the possibility of separately assessed components with the statement 'the assessment is criterion-referenced', but thirteen groups gave no answer to this question, without explanation because (it may be supposed) their schemes were not assessed in components.

More common ground seems to exist, though nothing approaching unanimity, over the uses to which the language is to be put. Many schemes link the syllabus directly to demands which grow according to the situation in which the pupil is to deploy the language s/he has learnt, for example by using a day trip as the basis for level 1, a more extended visit with a group for level 2 and a stay with a family for level 3. There are again many variations in the ways in which language needed for these purposes is specified, but the idea of an expanding social context for the individual's language use is common to many groups.

This is also the most frequent basis for grading, but some groups explain the levels in other ways. The material for each level can be recommended by the group as sufficient for one year's work for good or average pupils, and at the same time as suitable for a term's work for a top set and one and a half years for slower pupils, with possibilities for ancillary courses in the sixth form. Another way of differentiating levels is by increasing the areas covered: three topic areas at level 1, five at level 2, nine at level 3 and so on, and in addition more demanding requirements for personal conversational contacts and reading. In this case each level includes the requirements for the previous one and adds more. Alternatively a scheme can propose a wide range of functions from the beginning and recycle them at each level with more complex exponents, adding only a few new ones each time. This is justified by the multiplicity of ways in which the same idea can be expressed, for example from a direct and somewhat blunt request to an indirect and tactful enquiry, depending on the resources of the learner, the relationship between the speakers and the circumstances in which the communication takes place.

Test types follow on from the principle of an ever-widening context for language use, with comprehension tests of listening and reading, or sometimes both in the same test, relating to what is heard or read in the context of a visit to the country concerned, for example hearing announcements about the time of arrival of the boat at Boulogne, conversational exchanges about buying souvenirs, finding the way, ordering food and

22

drink and so on; and for reading, shop names, notices and signs. The simplest way to assess these receptive skills of listening and reading comprehension (though not the easiest way to write tests) is by objective items, usually in multiple-choice format. Several of the groups' notes for teachers point out that the use of English in the options is justified by the need to ensure that the assessment must relate more to the foreign language as heard or read than to understanding the mechanics of answering. In some schemes there are also a number of short answers in English, either objective (a number, yes/no, translation of one word) or open-ended (What does he want? Where is she going?), usually mixed in among multiple-choice items. True/false items also appear occasionally. The use of visuals is common to both in listening (maps connected with street directions, objects to be bought and/or eaten, numbers for dates or prices, clock faces) and in reading (shop fascias, signs, notices).

Most speaking tests consist of personal questions about family, likes and dislikes and interests, followed by a role-playing exercise in which the teacher takes one part and the candidate the other, with varying degrees of guidance and interaction for each. There is a perennial difficulty in explaining to the candidate what s/he is to talk about without supplying English instructions which are virtually translated (Ask me where the station is. Where is the station?). The reaction against translation as a technique for learning results in efforts to avoid it, but most groups seem to accept it as inevitable and it is occasionally written into the test, for example by directing the candidate to change the English in a printed conversation with the examiner into spoken French. Other schemes argue that in practice pupils will know more of the foreign language than their parents when they go abroad and can therefore be expected to act as interpreters in simple situations. But there is no doubt that in a role play there is a considerable problem in putting into the candidate's mind what s/he is to express in the foreign language, and the commonest solution is pictures, either individually on cue cards or in a set on a sheet, sometimes to stimulate the necessary vocabulary and sometimes to provide a context for what is to be said.

The controls set for speaking tests range from carefully written instructions for both halves of the conversation to a free exchange limited only by the need to solve a problem set (e.g. lost bag – police station – what was in it?). In a few speaking tests the assessment is not based on a teacher–pupil conversation but an exchange between pupils, usually controlled by cue cards and/or pictures, and sometimes by real objects.

23

Writing in the foreign language is usually not tested until later on, and then usually takes the form of a letter in response to one received from a pen friend.

Several groups have a separate assessment of background, by which is meant an appreciation of the differences between life in the foreign country and in Britain (stamps at a tobacco counter in France, the difference between a tram stop and a bus stop in Germany). This is usually assessed by means of multiple-choice tests and/or pictures. In most schemes, however, it is regarded as essential but incidental content in the other tests.

The target groups for most of the mathematics schemes are specifically those of lower ability, since the certificates are intended to be evidence for potential employers of basic arithmetic competence or numeracy. The research in science is directed at all abilities, starting at the top. The examinations in performing arts are in theory available to all comers, though a filtering process operates in the fact that pupils are presented for the examination by their teachers. The certificates for sport are awarded to a very high proportion of entrants, but again they are entered by instructors who are therefore in control of the awards.

The successful completion of a series of closely defined tasks in communicative situations has implications which can be illustrated by reference to assessments in other areas. Any test can be regarded as a single task made up of a series of smaller ones. The special meaning to be attached to the word 'task' in the context of graded tests is the application of what has been learnt to achieving some end rather than using it for the completion of testing exercises, which show only that knowledge or skill has been acquired. In that case, a piece of music performed for an examiner would be a task, and a scale or arpeggio an exercise. Similar contrasts can be found in dance (set exercises: placing of arms .../set dances: Highland Fling); mathematics ($12 \times 16 = ?$/How many carpet tiles 1 ft square do you need for a room 12 ft wide and 16 ft long?); shorthand (50 selected words ... short forms of *altogether, February, insurance* .../ ... a business letter) and of course in languages (... appropriate speech for a role left blank in dialogue read with examiner/... hold a conversation).

Examiner judgement is a perennial problem in all task-oriented tests unless the marking is done entirely objectively, as it sometimes is for example in swimming (Swim continuously for two minutes using any stroke, or strokes, without contact with bath wall or floor) or football

(Kick the ball to your partner so that it doesn't touch the ground in the square, between you, which is empty. Score: 5 out of 10 tries). The criteria for these assessments are nearly always written down as instructions, but most organizations, as well as setting high standards of qualification, demand that examiners attend various forms of training or briefing meetings (sometimes every year as a condition of appointment) and sometimes that they should conduct their first examinations under supervision by a senior examiner (music, spoken English, languages). Task-oriented tests occur in some language examinations, but more rarely (given the above definition) than might be expected now that communicative tests, starting with role plays but extending into problem-solving, appear in EFL and spoken English syllabuses as well as the newer examinations in French. They have existed for many years already in the examinations of the English Speaking Board (ESB; 1953) and the Institute of Linguists (1969 syllabus). Both these independent boards have always regarded language as a means to other ends rather than (or as well as) a study in itself, the former as a vital developmental skill, the latter as a professional skill. Tasks are more frequent in music and speech and drama, but not universal, as the examples above show. Award and test schemes in sport (football, hockey, swimming) are built up almost entirely of tasks to be done, either a given number of times within a set time limit or a set number of successes among a given number of attempts, or scoring points for relative distances a ball is hit. An exception to this generally objective approach is in diving, where a short statement on 'standard' contains five subjective judgements: 'The dives to be of a *reasonable* standard, giving *good* stance, *some* height in take off, a *recognizable* position during flight and a *neat* entry.'

The momentum gained by GOML schemes is largely a result of new motivation for pupils. The close link between the content of the course and the content of the test means that they become part of the same process: learning. All tests are motivating to a certain extent, but here pupils do not take the tests until they are likely to pass, so that when success does come (and for some pupils a level 1 certificate may be the first tangible proof of success they have ever had at school) they are spurred on to try for level 2. In other subjects there is little evidence of the same close link. The tests tend to set the pattern for teaching rather than stimulate it positively in new directions, except perhaps in similarly communicative language examinations (Royal Society of Arts, London Chamber of Commerce, Trinity College). The point is that GOML tests are a special case (as ESB were twenty-five years ago) of tests stimulating a new approach to teaching rather than consolidating the more timid methods of current practice. The only parallels outside languages seem to be in sports, where the football and hockey schemes were designed specifically to stimulate interest in the relevant game, and in mathematics, where tests are regularly built into the learning scheme (KMP) or accumulate over a period (Redditch).*

* For descriptions of these and other test schemes in mathematics, see Appendix C.

IV. Certificates and public examinations

Those most interested in GOML certificates are the pupils awarded them, and through pupils, parents (Table 17). In keeping with the principle that the rewards are for the individual's satisfaction, certificates are less often used as evidence for other users within the school or outside it, and information given to parents and published in newsletters and local papers relates more to the success of the schemes in terms of learning and achievement than to the qualifications they provide. They are in any case strictly local, usually endorsed by the LEA, and not often by any other body (Table 18), though LEA endorsement has sometimes required lengthy negotiation.

The content of the certificate varies considerably. In general, separate assessments for different components and other forms of profile reporting are not recorded (Table 19), but on the back of most certificates there is some kind of explanation or description of what the award implies (Table 20). The trends which are apparent from these global figures – that most explanations are given in terms of skills and abilities and that these explanations are more related to activities than to skills when it comes to describing what is certified – conceal a wide variation in the wording of certification. In an *ad hoc* sample of ten certificates the following wordings appear on the front: 'This certificate has been awarded to X'; 'X has passed the ... certificate'; 'X has achieved a pass/credit'; 'X has reached the required standard'; 'X has successfully completed the ... test'; 'X has been awarded a pass'; and no statement at all, merely the heading and the pupil's name. The description 'achievement' appears on four of these certificates, 'proficiency' on two, and 'test' or 'examination' without further qualification of this kind on three. It may seem pedantic to discuss precise wordings on certificates, but this is one way of approaching the problem of exactly what a graded test system is and what results can be expected from it. More detailed information is usually given on the back of these certificates (though in two of the ten samples there is none). Here again there is considerable variation, from reference to a defined syllabus of words and phrases to a more functional approach which declares broadly 'the French needed to ...', or specifies more precisely a set of

27

criteria which are constant but are performed better at each stage of testing: 'more communicative ability, greater accuracy, a wider range of grammar and vocabulary, more fluency and the ability to cope with longer and more complex stretches of language'. Most certificates specify either topic areas (the classroom, shopping) or functions (asking the way, buying a stamp) but again the complexity of description varies from five simple headings for level 1 (travel, café, shopping, town, accommodation) to thirty lines or so of activities for the scheme as a whole of which most are covered for the first level. Even within functional descriptions there is a range of precision from 'asking the time' to 'enquire about and express simple feelings and attitudes'. The most frequent topics among these ten schemes are shopping (eight), asking the way (eight), going to a café or restaurant (seven) and giving personal details (seven). In spite of this common ground, however, it seems that the concept of a 'defined syllabus' is interpreted in many different ways by the different groups.

Other principles implied by the idea of graded tests are involved in grading. If the assessment is concerned with the individual pupil's performance of specified tasks, it is appropriate to apply criterion-referencing procedures in the tests. Two principles of criterion-referenced assessment are first the definition of criteria either as individual objectives or as domains and second the illogicality of adding up marks resulting from the assessment of different, and by definition unlike, criteria. The evidence from the responses to the questionnaire (Table 21) is that these principles are not strictly applied by GOML schemes in practice. A variation on the 'did/didn't' assessments implicit in criterion-referencing is practised by one group which differentiates between stages (the point at which a test is taken) and levels (the result of judgement on a performance) so that a candidate who reaches high levels at a given stage can legitimately qualify for a credit because the performance goes beyond what is expected at that stage. Only one other scheme reports a similar approach, though it is differently applied, being based on an accumulation of credits over a period.

The use of certificates in other areas (music, mathematics and so on) varies considerably, depending on the purposes of the assessment. Some schemes have no certificates of their own but confirm progress in the subject at regular intervals up to an existing examination, or an alternative version of one (KMP to GCE Mode II, Redditch to CSE Mode III). Alternatively, there may be no certificate at all because the scheme is concerned with the motivation of the pupils and the help teachers can provide as a result of the assessments (Wiltshire). Other local schemes have certificates very like some of the GOML ones, listing topics covered (Hertfordshire) or a detailed syllabus (Norton). The certificates for music can be regarded either as evidence of a personal achievement, with some reflected glory for the teacher (who is mentioned on it) or as support for an application for entry to one of the schools of music or as a qualification for partial exemption from GCE. Sports certificates are almost entirely personal achievements, though some have social significance (survival swimming, life-saving) and others might, even if unofficially, be regarded as qualifications for team selection.

Grading is usually either an annotation on the certificate, as it is for GCE (e.g. pass/credit/distinction in music and the performing arts) or represented in a series of certificates, one for each grade as the GOML ones are (e.g. sports) – or sometimes both, with endorsements for higher levels on a certificate already awarded for the first grade (Norton, Judgemeadow). At first sight this distinction between a series of grades on a certificate and a series of certificates for successive grades might seem to be one of the crucial differences between the once-only, 'big bang' examination at the end of the course and the shorter-term assessments taken by the pupil when s/he is ready to pass. But the differences in the way the results are arrived at are not at all clear-cut. In music, for example, the grades are awarded by the examiner at the time of the examination, because s/he knows what the pass mark is for each section of the examination, and uses that as a starting point from which to add or deduct marks according to the quality of the performance. Adding enough marks will result in a higher-level award. The same system is used by the English Speaking Board and the Institute of Linguists in its oral examinations. The GCE boards, however, set standards for the examination only when all the marking is over, and take into account the experience of the examiners during the marking, last year's examination and the statistics resulting from this year's in arriving at decisions about grades. Yet both examinations issue much the same certificate in principle: in the case of music, one of the categories pass/credit/distinction, and in the case of GCE, one of the grades A to E. The differences between the two systems are not so much in the form of the certificates as in their availability and the length of learning time they represent.

Another distinction which is claimed to separate the graded test approach and that of the once-only public examinations is that the former can be reported as a profile of performances in different parts of the examination, whereas the GCE results are monolithic. The SLAPONS and Judgemeadow schemes in mathematics both report a level on each of a series of different sections, and represent the result as a histogram. The same principle is applied in the return to candidates of mark forms with comments (performing arts and music, and also Pitman's shorthand) which are intended to explain to them what was good and what was bad about their performance. These are not part of the certification, but a kind of unofficial bonus. But a similar system is operated with the grades given for oral examinations in GCE O-level languages and in addition, at A level, for some science practicals. The information is less detailed, but the principle is the same.

Yet, in spite of these overlaps and similarities in procedure, there seems to be total incompatibility between graded tests, as conceived and put into effect by GOML groups, and the public examinations. GOML tests form a progressive system of short-term goals based on a mastery-learning philosophy which should predicate criterion-referenced assessments resulting in success for nearly all candidates. GCE and CSE examinations result in certificates awarded at the end of a five-year course and use procedures which are based on norm-referencing, usually allocating the top three grades to rather over half the candidates (GCE) or spreading candidates out on either side of a postulated average for all pupils of the same age (CSE).

Nevertheless, although only a few GOML groups are reported to have had candidates take a public examination (eight groups in all three languages for CSE and one in German for GCE), fifteen groups (40 per cent of respondents) were at the time of answering the questionnaire in negotiation with a public board about an examination in French and nearly 60 per cent (twenty-one) were aiming to link into CSE at some time in the future. The largest interest is in CSE alone, but this probably derives from the fact that pupils will reach the level of public examining before the new 16+ examination comes into operation.

There are two approaches among GOML groups to public examinations. The more purist view is that the nature of graded tests is such that there can never be any compatibility with the public examinations system, because the aims, methods and results in each case are totally different – in kind, not just in scale or application. If the new approach to language learning which is reflected in graded tests is good enough to stand the test of time, the argument runs, it will gain wider and wider acceptance on its own merits and the public examination system will come to be seen as inappropriate and will therefore have to change. Whether it changes or not, however, is no concern of GOML groups, who are providing local test systems for their own pupils and are not interested in wider issues of equivalence or national certification.

The second, more pragmatic view is that the public examination system has demonstrably not adapted itself sufficiently to new ideas in the teaching of modern languages over the last sixty years and that unless some positive action is taken by GOML interests to promote the development of new assessment procedures, the communicative approach to language learning will be restricted, or stifled entirely, by the backwash of inappropriate examinations. The principles of a functional methodology, it is argued, hold good from the beginning of language learning onwards, with development in different directions at the higher levels, but in principle without limit. But there is some fear that graded tests may eventually be limited by a switch-over to examination courses for the more able after levels 1–3, or by the use of graded tests from the beginning for lower-ability pupils only, for as many as may go on up to 16+. The first of these alternatives perpetuates the two-tier course in which the language is taught for the first three years and the examination syllabus is taught for the last two; the second implies that functional syllabuses are not a good enough basis for those of the brighter pupils who may be expected to take public examinations.

If these situations are to be avoided, the question arises of how the graded test approach can be reconciled with a public examination system which, as mentioned above, has a different approach to assessment. Only one CSE board has so far run a Mode III examination for a local GOML group (though other Mode III schemes are in advanced stages of discussion). The syllabus for this examination may help to show how the incompatibilities mentioned above are reconciled in practice. The first consideration is whether the progressive nature of the graded test scheme is carried forward into the CSE examination, whether there is evidence that this CSE examination is equivalent to a level 4 test in the GOML scheme. Although the CSE examination appears to be an end-of-course assessment, there are in fact two elements in it, one of which covers a longer span. The regional assessment is made on the once-only examination towards the end of the fifth year, but the school assessment is cumulative, building up on a series of tests over the last five complete terms of the course (i.e. from the beginning of the fourth year). This series cannot, however, be considered as one of graded tests because the teacher assessors

31

are instructed to mark into the set of grades used for the examination as a whole, which, in accordance with the definitions laid down nationally for CSE certificates, are specifically norm-referenced ('Grade 4 is to be awarded to candidates whose attainment in the subject is what one would expect of an average 16-year-old'). Further, this means that candidates are not entered when they are ready (in the GOML sense of 'ready to show mastery'), and resulting certificates in 1979 recorded all grades from 1 to 5. The examination does not therefore follow the principles of GOML as exemplified in the quotation from Harding *et al.* given in Chapter I. However, one principle which is to a certain extent put into practice is testing by tasks, since the syllabus does define situations in which candidates will be expected to communicate (or in terms of the syllabus, 'survive') and lists the topics on which s/he is to be able to converse with a French person, but the content of the narrative text to be read is not specified, and the writing of a short story on a picture series could not be regarded as functional. Another sense in which the syllabus is in line with GOML principles is that it is a local development tailored to the local scheme, but this will no longer apply if the syllabus is borrowed for other schemes, and this appears to be imminent.

Information received from the CSE boards indicates that two of them have approved in principle Mode III syllabuses proposed by GOML groups; two have been approached with proposals; one has set up a study group to consider the problems presented by the graded test approach; one is already conducting its own review of syllabuses and one will introduce a new Mode I syllabus in 1983 which has been influenced by GOML thinking. Another board is involved in a feasibility study which has just reached level 1. Two boards mention that graded tests will be taken into account in discussions about the new 16+ examination. There is no indication yet how the problems of compatibility between the aims of CSE and of GOML schemes are being solved, but it does not seem likely that they will prove any less intractable than they did for the Mode III examination already operating. The moderator's report for 1979 says that 'the evidence of this year's examination would appear to suggest that this level of the Graded Examination and CSE are not incompatible', but it is legitimate to ask from the GOML point of view at what price this compatibility has been bought. There are some gains – explicitly communicative aims and new definitions for the syllabus – but the need for discrimination, which is emphasized in the moderator's report, has altered the nature of the assessments from confirmation of achievement for most candidates to a sorting of performances into categories of relative success, which results in deliberately arranged shortfall for all but a few.

Most GCE boards have not so far been directly involved in graded test developments, mainly because they appear to be awaiting the outcome of the present discussions about the new examination structure before considering any new syllabuses. One of the GCE research units, however, has been analysing past GCE and CSE scripts to try to establish grade criteria for the new 16+ examination on the basis of actual candidate performance. This may provide useful information in discussions about what candidates should be capable of, but a modern language has not yet been tackled, and when it is the conclusions may not be applicable in a new situation where syllabuses may be radically different from before. One of the boards has commissioned working groups to look at the implications of a graded test approach for modern languages at 16+, and this is directly related to the linking of GOML tests into the public examination system. The suggestion is that a candidate's grade should be awarded on a points system deriving from his or her performance on some or all of a set of units which would include tests of the four skills at two levels. A minimum number of units would have to be taken if a certificate was to be awarded at all, and all units would have to be taken if the candidate was to qualify for the top grades. This principle of accumulation of credits seems a promising way forward, and indeed is very similar to the system on which the Redditch Mode III examination in mathematics is already organized. Knitting the two systems together in this way would result in the adaptation of public examinations to modern teaching methods, and if the functional approach to languages adopted by GOML groups were to be carried forward into it, it would put into practice a principle which modern language teachers have been arguing with little effect since the 1930s – that the examinations should reflect good teaching methods rather than shape courses with efficient methods of assessment.

If a useful relationship is to be established between GOML tests and the new 16+ examinations, a number of problems will have to be solved. These were discussed at a meeting organized by the GOML Coordinating Committee and CILT at Leeds in June 1981, and the discussions are reported in *GOML Newsletter* No. 5 (August 1981), of which an extract is quoted in Appendix D to this report. In summary, the problems concern the equivalence of levels in different GOML groups; the grading system of the new 16+ examination and the relationship of GOML levels to it; the availability of GOML level tests and the new examinations to all age groups; and the change-over from local GOML level tests to the national examination system for individual pupils when they reach the stage at which they need terminal rather than interim certification.

The solutions proposed are logically feasible but will require a great deal of flexibility from both GOML groups and the 16+ consortia. For example the GOML groups will have to agree to some kind of national calibration, which most seem so far to be unwilling to accept because it threatens central control of essentially autonomous, local schemes. For the examining boards the proposal that 16+ grades should start at 1 and work up to 7 rather than the reverse, which would be a powerful move towards an open-ended view of education, is unlikely to be acceptable for modern languages alone, and teachers and administrators in other subjects may need some persuading to see it as an important enough innovation to be adopted universally. Again, the proposition that the new examination should be open to all learners at any age who are ending their language study (perhaps only for the time being), so that they can finish with a certificate of attainment at the appropriate level, means that the boards will have to be prepared to accept 12- and 13-year-olds as candidates for parts of the examination (e.g. grades 6 and 7 as representing levels 1 and 2 of GOML schemes).

These may seem at first sight to be such revolutionary proposals that they are hardly worth considering in the context of a new 16+ examination. But there is no logical objection to them in principle: a national examination system could be set up in this way and work administratively as well as the present system, and educationally much more positively. The real problem is that a national examination system is not being designed, it is being developed from two existing systems. The implications of this are discussed further in Chapter VII.

V. Characteristics of systems

The last three chapters have discussed facts about GOML groups and any similarities and differences which could be established between them and other systems of testing and examining. It is now time to describe GOML schemes in qualitative terms, reporting what those most directly involved think about them and estimating how far they measure up to the ideals they are intended to embody. In addition, since this report has inevitably drawn most of its information from those who have worked hardest to promote GOML schemes, some account should be given of criticisms which have been made of the GOML approach. Finally, comparisons with schemes in other subjects are introduced again with some subjective comments from their originators on how they work in practice.

The questionnaire sent out to GOML groups asked for the opinions of those involved on the character of the group – the affective aspects of GOML. Summaries of the responses (Tables 22–5) were drawn up to show all the points mentioned, with a note of the number of responses for each when more than one. The highest number of responses (96) relate to successes (Table 22), which is some indication of the enthusiasm of groups for the new approach. On the other hand the highest number of points mentioned is in connection with distinctive features of groups (51), even though the response rate overall is lower (65) (Table 23). This seems to support the view that the individuality of groups is considered important – and actual – by those involved, even though several of the features considered distinctive (e.g. most of those in the first section of the list) are common to most groups. The essential conclusion here is not that the groups may be wrong in what they consider to be distinctive about their own work but that they feel that they are in command of the situation, that they have established a scheme for themselves and that they are encouraged by their own achievements. What that achievement is can be judged from Table 22, where pupil motivation and/or enthusiasm is by far the most frequently mentioned success resulting from the schemes (32 responses). It is significant that the total mentions of positive results for pupils (the first section on the list, numbering 48) is higher than that of positive results for teachers (second section, 35), though the two are clearly very closely linked. The problem points (Table 24) number about the same as the successes, but the responses are about a third fewer. The largest category of problems is related to physical and administrative constraints such as finding sufficient time, support and money (which in a sense are all aspects of the same problem). Reaching agreement on the content of the scheme is mentioned, but is evidently not considered a major difficulty: this may be a reflection either of the self-evident benefits of the new approach or the fact that groups consist largely of volunteers. Finally, the question on ideal assessments (Table 25) produced only 45 responses, perhaps because more respondents than actually said so agreed with the statement that 'this is not an ideal world', but more likely because the results of GOML groups' schemes have been above all practical. They have gained momentum because they *work*, and this makes the considerable effort required to produce them worthwhile. (What 'work' means in this context will be discussed in Chapter VII.)

At the beginning of the present investigation a definition of the concept 'graded test' was set up on the basis of the quotation from Harding *et al.* given in Chapter I: it means a test system which is progressive, task-oriented and linked into the learning process. If these are the ideals, how far, judging by the information received from the questionnaire, are they put into practice in GOML schemes?

All the schemes are certainly progressive, in that each level adds more material to the last, either horizontally in range (for example by increasing the number of topics or the amount of vocabulary specified) or vertically in depth by recycling the functions which have been exemplified at the lower levels. In every case each level includes and builds on the previous one, though there is never any suggestion that the earlier-level tests must be taken before the later ones. To this extent the principle of setting tests at relatively short intervals is carried forward into practice. The only real problem is the resulting pressure on the production of test materials: once embarked on the series, with pupils moving up the levels and keen to continue, a group has to ensure that the next level will be ready for use when it is needed. The difficulty is of course increased for any central coordinating organization if several working parties are producing material in different languages in parallel.

The question of whether GOML tests make task-oriented assessments is much more complex. The phrase 'criterion-referenced' was avoided in the formulation used for the working hypothesis because it was likely to

36

narrow down the concept to a technical issue relating only to the construction and operation of tests.

There is some difficulty for the uninitiated in defining criterion-referenced assessment because it seems to be one of those technical terms which can be used to cover a range of concepts from a simple judgement on a performance ('types at 40 words per minute' – 41 words by the stopwatch is 'can' and 39 is 'can't') to a set of multiple-choice items on a domain of performance tasks related to a conceptual framework of subject content. Brown defines it as follows:

Criterion-referenced assessment provides information about the specific knowledge and abilities of pupils through their performance on various kinds of tasks that are interpretable in terms of what pupils know or can do, without reference to the performance of others.[10]

The GOML interpretation of criterion-reference seems to be more restricted than this because it is linked with the performance of language acts, which are realized in communicative tasks, rather than with knowledge of the language, which is generally taken to mean knowledge (not application) of structure and vocabulary. It is a question of 'can do' rather than 'knows'. But it also goes further than the definition given above because it includes the specification of objectives. Some authorities maintain that criterion-referenced assessment necessarily includes the specification of objectives, but this means either that subject specialists have to become expert at psychometrics or that testing experts have to specialize in every subject for which they set up test systems. The clash between testing theory and the practical assessment of language in use (a theme discussed in Harrison, 1977) indicates that there is usually a considerable tension between the best learning systems and the best testing systems.

This view is placed in a wider context by Brown:

There appears to be a crucial gap in the thinking about attainment and assessment. On the one hand, the behaviourists and measurement specialists have been able to lay down clear and explicit criteria for what constitutes a 'good' test ... they assume that they will be presented with schemes of behaviours by subject specialists (and others), and that then the real, technological job of test construction can start with the nature of that job being largely independent of the subject-matter involved. On the other hand, philosophers *are* concerned with questions of 'what it means to know or to learn' but for the most part do not discuss the implications of this for pupils' overt behaviour. In my view, there is a need to bridge this gap.[11]

GOML groups have begun to build bridges across the gap from the learning side, and though they may be short on testing theory, they are developing test materials which are improved continually as experience accumulates. The evidence for this is clear in the work of many schemes, but one particular example is the difference between Oxfordshire Modern Languages Achievement Certificate 1 (1978) and 2 (1981).

Most GOML groups which have written full test specifications set them out in behavioural terms, that is, using a form of statement for each objective which explains what the candidate is to perform. This is consistent with the new approach to language learning, but it must be admitted that the actual form of the tests often belies it. In a communication between two people through the medium of language, the four traditional language skills are not separable, as the titles of tests such as 'listening comprehension', 'reading comprehension', 'speaking' and 'writing' imply. It is only for convenience of categorization that tests are so labelled. To a large extent it is a legacy from the period when testing theory maintained that in order to know what was being assessed it was essential to isolate it, though even then it was recognized that the language tests were only *mainly* of listening or whatever. A functional approach to testing language would welcome this inevitable mixture of the four skills, together with others such as the recognition of role (e.g. the applications of 'tu' and 'vous' in French or the differing languages used by the same person in different circumstances); the interpretation of body language (e.g. facial expression and gesture); and the significance of context (e.g. visual clues to meaning, physical circumstances). The assessment's main concern is then appropriateness, and the test situations set up are in effect tasks in which problems are to be solved by the use of language. The syllabus therefore sets out the aspects of language which are needed to communicate successfully – the criteria for a criterion-referenced assessment.

These criteria have to be accurately defined for reasons of both validity and reliability. To achieve validity, the assessment must reflect as exactly as possible the content of the test syllabus. In a functional language test the candidate is asked to show that s/he has understood the meaning of something s/he has read (for example the name of a shop: boulangerie/poissonnerie) or something s/he has heard (directions to the post office), and these are of course exactly what the syllabus specifies both as functions (reading common signs, understanding spoken directions) and topics (shopping, town). The difficulty is in evolving test procedures which enable the candidate to show what s/he has understood without involving him/her in non-communicative activities. It seems consistent with the situation in which these language activities would occur in real life for the candidate to be told s/he is looking for a baker's shop and then shown a picture of a row of shop fronts among which s/he is to choose one, but in real life there would be different objects on display in the different windows and the tourist would probably not need to understand the meaning of the *words* 'boulangerie' and 'poissonnerie'. The directions to the post office would almost certainly be accompanied by gestures and a good deal more language from both parties to the exchange than the bald statement usually heard on the listening comprehension tape. The use of text plus multiple-choice items for 'comprehension' tests sacrifices context to precision.

If these criteria are a series of tasks, the presentation of results should ideally be in the form of a performance rating on each of them, unless they can be considered as parts of a single coherent 'domain'. Whether they are separately defined criteria or domains, the 'did/didn't' assessments on each criterion or domain cannot be added together to give a composite score. This influences both the specification (How finely can the components of a task be described, and which of them can be grouped together?) and the reporting of results (For how many different categories can a level of attainment be stated?). The result of a criterion-referenced test should be a profile of achievements on different criteria as specified in the syllabus.

In the light of this discussion it should now be possible to decide how far GOML schemes are in practice using criterion-referenced assessment as they originally aimed to do.[12] The answer is, not very far. They are often task-oriented in the wider sense proposed, particularly in the specifications of objectives. At the other end of the process, many speaking tests are marked on a system which sets a premium on communication, so that it would be possible to publish a criterion-referenced assessment for a speaking test alone. But nearly all schemes test listening and reading with multiple-choice items, a format which is incompatible with a criterion-referenced approach. Very few schemes offer a profile result, and most set a pass mark which is a totalling of all scores over all tests, suitably weighted. A listing of topics on the certificate does not alter the fact that the language used to fulfil them is described in terms of skills. The certificate is then a record of a standard set and achieved, rather than activities successfully completed. It is obvious, however, that this mismatch between theory and practice does not affect the revitalizing impact of GOML schemes. For the pupils and the teachers involved, 30 grams of successful practice is worth a tonne of theory.

The third element in the working hypothesis definition of a graded test was that it is an integral part of the learning process. Again the answer is yes and no. The motivational effect of GOML schemes, both on pupils and teachers, has evidently been enormous (Table 22), and to this extent the new approach has already made a great contribution to language learning. But the phrase was also intended to include the diagnostic use of the tests to show both pupil and teacher how well the individual's learning is progressing, and although informal discussions about the results of the tests do obviously take place, use of the test as a promotion of individualized learning has apparently not happened, as much for organizational reasons as any other. But without a more individual result, such as would be provided by profile reporting, there is little evidence available of what remedial action is suitable. Again theory is overtaken by practical considerations, and the lack of specific feedback from the tests does not seem to be considered important.

So far the evidence considered in this report has all been from the committed: there is no doubt about the viability and value of GOML in the minds of those involved. There have been some criticisms, however, ranging from theoretical dismissal to journalistic rhetoric, with some reasoned discussion of practical problems between these extremes. The theoretical objections are that if performance is the only justification for language teaching the pupils will not have any understanding of how the language works as a mechanism. The purpose of language teaching should be 'to develop the pupil's awareness of language, to mature his innate capacity for language ...' – a linguistic justification rather than a practical one, since pupils do not have 'needs' for foreign languages, and the communicative approach gives them skills they will never use.[13] A less thoughtful attack suggests that the graded test approach may encourage the lower ability pupils, but does not suit the bright ones. The argument is not enhanced by constant overstatement, but two points do emerge: the dangers of lack of generative capacity and the problem of error.[14] These are difficulties which GOML groups are well aware of, since they have direct experience of putting their principles into practice. The polemic is answered by the leader of a group: the barriers complained of are those set up by outmoded assessment procedures, and the groups are working 'to re-establish foreign languages as a viable subject on the comprehensive-school curriculum'.[15]

40

Other dangers which have been mentioned are squeezing out 'aspects of language study which are not measured by performance tests, such as understanding ... of the foreign country ...' and 'limiting what is done by the abler pupils'. The answer to both these is probably the same, that an approach through needs does not limit the provision to performance objectives alone or to material for one group of learners only: on the contrary, it allows the content of the course to be more precisely geared to the requirements of all learners, once it has been decided what these are. There is also the practical difficulty of arranging for tests to be taken by individual pupils when they are ready rather than by classes, which means that the tests are 'too easy for some and beyond the capacity of others'. This is an organizational problem for schools which cannot be solved without a commitment to individualized teaching and therefore vertical grouping, which is dependent on agreement across subjects and cannot be solved by modern language teachers alone.

In other subjects the main evidence available of subjective evaluation by users is in mathematics. Here the same themes emerge as in GOML evaluations but with a greater emphasis (as might be expected) on employer involvement. The success of schemes depends on setting realistic, short-term goals within the capabilities of the learners, and some schemes emphasize the importance of individualized learning as a way of giving pupils of all abilities the opportunity to develop their potential. On the other hand a few schemes were devised with lower-ability (or 'non-academic') pupils in mind. The positive achievements of pupils can give them strong motivation to learn more, and can also give them a more positive attitude altogether to mathematics as a subject. The involvement of teachers and advisers in setting up schemes has obviously been of vital importance and also the commitment of the individual teacher to the scheme in his or her work with the class. The diagnostic value of the tests is also mentioned as one of their main practical advantages. In several cases one of the main reasons for setting up the scheme in the first place was to provide information for employers and two of them result in easily interpreted profiles of achievement. In another the prospective employer can influence the emphasis of the course for individuals by stating what the demands for particular jobs are, and in another there is provision for a more general exchange of information between employers and teachers about the equation of courses and employment. A fuller account of these views is included in Appendix C.

In sum, the success of schemes in general lies in teacher commitment and pupil involvement. The systems as they have been developed, mainly by teachers, are designed to set pupils tasks which they can see to be relevant to real life and in small enough instalments for them to achieve success and, through success, motivation for the next instalment. The tests are therefore an indispensable component of the schemes because they show all concerned – pupil, teacher, employer, parent – that what has been achieved is a positive contribution to the pupil's development.

VI. Transferability

As might be expected, the principles of language learning and testing which are appropriate for modern languages in secondary schools are likely to be suitable for English as a foreign language (EFL) and as a second language (ESL) in Great Britain. (The distinction between these two is that EFL is applied to the teaching of visitors who are only temporarily resident in the country whereas ESL is the English needed by permanent residents whose native language is not English.) But tests of the communicative use of language in EFL are mainly achievement tests set by examining bodies external to schools and taken at the end of courses (Royal Society of Arts, Association of Recognized English Language Schools orals) and testing for diagnostic purposes is usually undertaken within the individual school or group of schools. Much the same situation exists with ESL, where achievement is assessed by CSE examinations (North West CSE Board and occasional Mode III syllabuses) and informal checks are included in course material. In neither case has there been any development similar to GOML schemes, with groups of teachers working on short-term objectives marked by progressive tests, but there could be, especially since organizations exist in both fields which could run tests of this kind if there was a demand for them.

The principles established by GOML could also be applied to the learning and testing of foreign languages in Europe – English, French, German and so on, depending on the country. There is already considerable cross-reference between modern language teachers in Europe (including Great Britain) through the interaction network set up by the Modern Languages Project of the Council of Europe, which has promoted visits of language teachers and others from one country to another and encouraged the exchange of ideas and information. This means that there is already proof of the transferability of a communicative or notional/functional approach to language learning from one situation to another. Nevertheless the development of local schemes of the GOML type, conceived and organized by groups of teachers and concerned with short-term goals, is rare – or possibly unique, depending on the criteria used to define a 'GOML-type' scheme. Communicative teaching materials are becoming more and more common, but testing techniques lag some way behind. Development work on new kinds of tests is going on at universities in various countries and new achievement tests are being prepared for schools by nationally funded projects, sometimes in a whole range of subjects, not just in languages. But though there are many parallels, such as the involvement of teachers, the use of objectives-based tests and a concern with language used for communicative purposes, there does not seem to be much likelihood of a direct transfer of GOML principles to other European situations. This is because the conditions in which it has grown – a need for a new approach for pupils who had not previously been expected to learn a foreign language and a certain freedom of curriculum coupled with a demanding national examinations system – do not exist in quite the same way elsewhere.

On a narrower front, the question of transferability is whether GOML-type developments could be paralleled in other subjects. Certainly there are many schemes of various kinds in mathematics, as already discussed in earlier chapters and summarized in Appendix C, but less activity has been apparent so far in science. Various schemes are reported to be under way in different LEAs, but the only evidence discovered so far is the adaptation of the Manchester 'Science at Work' materials for a CSE Mode III submission. The most relevant parallel development is a proposal for a graded test scheme in science prepared at the ILEA's North London Science Centre. This draws on GOML experience of assessing short-term objectives and on the experimental work on cognitive levels in science mentioned earlier, but is perhaps most significant in its suggestion that a system of graded tests should be run by a single professional body, not local groups or the present examining boards. This is as bold a suggestion (and in much the same terms) as the 16+ proposals of the GOML meeting of June 1981 reported in the previous chapter. It may be more likely to succeed, to the extent that it represents an entirely new venture rather than the adaptation of an established system.

A distinction is commonly drawn in discussions about graded tests between 'progressive' subjects in which later learning is dependent on successful early learning, and other subjects which are more concerned with areas of knowledge and techniques for understanding and appreciating them. Examples of 'progressive' subjects are languages, mathematics and science and of 'areas' subjects history, geography and literature. The implication of this distinction is that the principles of graded tests are by definition applicable only to the progressive subjects, and cannot be transferred to the 'areas' subjects. Certainly no schemes have been reported in any subjects other than mathematics and science in answer to the enquiries made for this report. Rumours of graded schemes in domestic science in the Midlands have not been substantiated with evidence.

The crucial question seems to be what distinguishes an advanced learner from an intermediate learner in 'areas' subjects: s/he certainly knows more, but has also learnt how to use that knowledge to greater effect. This is similar to the difference between an advanced and intermediate language learner when taught by communicative methods, since s/he will first learn for example to ask (somewhat rigidly) for a meal or a hotel room, and later learn more subtle ways of expressing wants – an instance of that recycling of functions which is the basis of several GOML schemes. If this parallel can be accepted, the transfer of GOML-type procedures from progressive subjects to 'areas' subjects requires the definition of the uses to which known facts are put. The history pupil needs not only to know that 1914–18 = First World War but also appreciate the significance of that event in its context, just as the language pupil needs to know the meanings of words and the forms of sentences before s/he can relate the language s/he hears or speaks to the context in which it is used. This is probably too simplistic a comparison, but the concept of progression is a constant in learning, and grading (in the GOML sense) should therefore be possible in principle. A practical description of progressive objectives in 'area' subjects may, however, be impossible without returning to the abstract nouns of hierarchies of educational objectives, which are so difficult to realize in applied forms such as test papers.

As this discussion has shown, it is not easy to define what aspects of GOML schemes could helpfully be transferred to other situations and other subjects. If the need is great enough and the teachers determined enough, existing ideas can be adapted as necessary to meet the challenge. The only precondition is understanding of the existing ideas among potential adapters.

VII. Implications and conclusion

Like any other issue in education, the development of GOML schemes has implications for a wide range of interested parties – pupils, teachers, schools, LEAs, parents, employers and examining boards, and also of course for the subject itself, languages.

For pupils the positive effects are more practical results from learning, more interest in the subject and a better contribution from languages to general education, especially in awareness of national similarities and differences. The disadvantage could be that the pupils of higher ability could be sold short, not necessarily because of any inherent shortcomings in communicative language teaching but because the route to employment and higher education passes through an examination system which is at present incompatible with objectives of the GOML kind, though this situation could change.

For teachers the greatest gain has been a rethinking of aims, and this reappraisal is implied for the teachers of any other subjects which may follow a similar path. They have started from good classroom procedures and looked for means of assessing the results of better learning. They have not yet entirely succeeded in producing relevant tests, but they are making progress in a healthy direction, from learning to assessment rather than from the setting of standards to a consideration of how to achieve them. The greatest problem is that curriculum and test development of this size demands a very heavy commitment in terms of time and effort, and although this will diminish as test materials accumulate for future use, there is still the problem of review and renewal especially if, as has happened up to now, experience becomes the basis for improvement. A more immediate problem, perhaps, is the reluctance of teachers to embark on a new approach to language learning which is not reflected in public examinations. Teachers see it as their responsibility to pupils and parents to ensure that pupils' achievement is properly certificated and they are therefore unwilling to put the pupils' chances at risk. The social pressure towards success in examinations in Great Britain is such that the only answer is to change the syllabuses quite radically, which is one of the goals of many GOML groups.

46

For schools the implications of the GOML approach are (in view of the positive effects noted above) a better choice of subjects for all pupils, even though an excess of demand has been created in some schools; a greater status for languages as subjects which can be seen to be success-fully taught; and broader educational opportunities for pupils. The main implications on the negative side are organizational. If all subjects adopted a short-term objectives approach, with tests at the end of each stage, it would be difficult to envisage any time of day or evening when there were not pupils being tested somewhere in some subject. This is perhaps an exaggeration, because the time problem is particularly acute with languages, where there is a commitment to individual speaking tests. These take up considerable amounts of time both in class and out of it. In other subjects there is little demand for assessment by speaking – though perhaps there should be more of this kind of assessment than there is at present. The solutions to these problems might be the extension of exist-ing schemes by which other subjects (history, geography) are taught through the medium of the foreign language, and a greater absorption of assessment into normal class procedures rather than tending to divide it off in both concept and time as a separate issue from learning.

For LEAs the advantage is that GOML schemes promote better language learning, but they are quite expensive in a time of financial stringency, particularly in time spent by teachers and advisers. Relatively speaking, however, they are remarkably good value, mainly because of the willingness of teachers to spend their own time (and sometimes money, as in travelling expenses not reclaimed) on doing the necessary work. In several schemes teachers have been seconded to work on GOML develop-ments, but the present cuts in LEA spending have already reduced this contribution and may have a quite disastrous effect on some areas. It would be a great loss if this kind of cutback halted the momentum which has been built up in so many schemes and is now beginning to show such positive results.

The evidence on the reaction of parents is that their children's enthu-siasm is infectious and that they are happy to see such clear evidence of achievement. Whether their holidays abroad are in the event enlivened by contacts made through their children's language skills is less important than the possibility that their own attitude to other countries may be positively affected, almost at second hand.

The implications for employers are not yet evident, partly because not many pupils who have taken part in GOML schemes have reached school-leaving age and so the certificates have yet to be evaluated by employers, but more because employers on the whole seem to be much less interested in language skills than in other qualifications – for school leavers, basic numeracy (one of the main reasons for test schemes in mathematics) and, at higher levels, general education (in spite of numerous reports and conferences on the need for languages in industry).

The implications for examining boards have already been mentioned in Chapter IV. There is considerable determination within a number of GOML groups to revitalize public examining with a new approach which can be shown to have been successful in schools. But past experience has shown that however persuasive the arguments in favour of change in modern language examinations, it comes exceedingly slowly, and there is a danger that using the graded test axe to chop down the public examination tree may risk blunting its cutting edge.

Nevertheless the issue is wider than this. The two crucial issues might be labelled content and form. The content argument concerns modern languages alone, and relates to the validity and reliability of different test formats. For example oral tests have always been given less weight in public examinations than they ought to be (by common consent), on the grounds that they are too difficult to mark reliably enough. Multiple-choice tests on the other hand can be highly reliable but are not appropriate for the assessment of communicative performance, even receptively. The boards are likely to give priority to making their examination results as reliable as possible, which they are persuaded is their prime responsibility, rather than to reflecting more accurately than at present the purposes for which language is actually used in real life. But the balance is a delicate one and it is time that some of the techniques developed in GOML groups and elsewhere were incorporated, after suitable trials, into public examination syllabuses.

The issue of form has already been mentioned in connection with the proposals for grading upwards from 1 to 7 (Appendix D). This concerns all subjects, since it is hardly feasible to implement two different kinds of grading for the same examination system. Support for this method of grading comes from well-established and widely used scales of attainment in EFL and the proposed graded test scheme in science (see Chapter VI). In spite of this evidence of practicality, there will inevitably be considerable resistance to the idea of overturning an established educational hierarchy of 'first is best' which traditionally runs from being top of the first form at school to the award of a First Class Honours degree. In the present

48

world, however, the notions of rapid change, permanent education and school as the foundation for learning (rather than the end of it) are the ones with which a new examination system should be grappling, even if they have already become clichés. Starting with level (or grade) 1 leaves the final level open and provides for a flexibility which a series of closed systems (O level, CSE, CEE, O/A, I level, A level ...) cannot accommodate. Starting at the bottom could alleviate the problems of grade definitions and equivalence because it could relate all developments in a subject to each other on a single scale.

The spread of GOML schemes into so many parts of the country and their difficulties in coping administratively with a growing demand suggest that the examination boards could, if they wished, begin to act as a service to teachers involved in assessment. This could be more than just a matter of providing programming facilities for local test statistics (though this would be valuable if organized as flexible help rather than fitting new figures into existing formulas) but embarking on full exploitation of the possibilities which will shortly become available. These could range from central storage of material in computer files which are accessible to each school in a group through its own equipment, to the printing of selected test materials on demand, the centralized amendment of materials in the light of experience and review, and even the keeping of pupil records by the pupils themselves.

The implications of the new approach for language learning as exemplified by the GOML schemes and others are applicable at all levels and for all language learners, since the principle of needs analysis is not confined to everyday applications (from shopping to engineering studies in the foreign language) but could be applied to the study of language as literature or even language as philosophy. The same question can be asked throughout: what for?

At a more prosaic level, GOML groups still have many problems to solve and one of the more worrying aspects of the developments so far is that the theories behind the schemes may never reach practical expression. Many issues have been difficult to resolve, and rather than hold up the progress of a scheme from design stage to realization in practice, some groups have put off central problems for later discussion. For example the principle that each pupil should be tested when s/he is ready to pass cannot be put into effect without some form of individualization in both learning and testing. This is possible, as the KMP project (among others) has shown, but it does not seem to have been tackled systematically in

GOML schemes: it depends on an integration of learning and assessment which has yet to be achieved in most groups. The problem of criterion-referenced assessment is another area of confusion and uncertainty, and the implications need thinking through before the present mixed system becomes embedded in a GOML tradition. Another question concerns the quality of the learning which the pupils experience. Some of them would not in the past have learnt a foreign language at all, and for them this is certainly more and better learning than otherwise. For those who without GOML would have been studying languages in a more traditional way, the question arises as to whether the new approach is a demanding enough intellectual experience. The answer is that it is probably not, but that it lays as good a foundation for future study of a more academic kind as that provided by a traditional approach; indeed, a better one, because more motivating. This is probable, but not yet proved, and needs to be monitored in some way.

These reservations do not diminish the considerable achievements of GOML groups so far, but they do point to a potential problem, that principles and theories, even though justifiably deferred in the rush to implementation, do in the end have to be put into practice or positively amended in the light of experience, otherwise the foundations will begin to slip and the reasons for doing things in a particular way will become remote and finally disappear, until in the end the new approach will seem to be little more than a rather weak variation on previous methods.

Nevertheless a communicative or functional approach to language learning represents a radical change of view. The use of language for communicative purposes, such as obtaining food and shelter or understanding a lecture on astrophysics, demands specifications of a new kind. Teachers have been searching for many years for some way of describing what is to be learnt which is consistent with the nature of language as a creative activity influenced by the context in which it is used. Lists of vocabulary and grammar, however rationally based, are illogical and restrictive: specification of language courses should concern itself with uses, not manipulations. The idea that the content of a course can be based on the purposes for which the learners will want to use the language does not sound particularly revolutionary, but it frees the syllabus from the grip of word counts and verb paradigms by specifying what communications are to be achieved with the language learnt and illustrating them with examples of the language which can be used for the purpose. The effect of this on tests is that they can begin to assess the ends rather than the means of language, concentrating on meanings rather than forms and approximating more nearly to reality, where appropriateness is more valuable than formal correctness. It is in carrying this principle through into curriculum development and assessment that GOML groups have broken new ground.

The most remarkable and encouraging aspect of GOML so far is that its success is based on the conviction and effort of teachers, who have taken as a starting point a practical problem of curriculum shortfall and found ways of solving it. Their enthusiasm and commitment has resulted in successful learning for pupils and improved morale for other teachers as well as themselves. The future development of GOML both vertically up the levels of learning and horizontally into other areas of the country is limited only by resources, both human and financial.

The experiences of language learning cannot be the same for all pupils. Mastery will be relative and any form of organization should attempt to take account of this and offer pupils the opportunity of success appropriate to their needs. For while there is as yet only limited evidence that the least able can be effectively motivated and achieve significant success, it is important to stress that they have rarely been set goals which are within their reach.[16]

They have now been set these goals – and within a system which can be applied to language learning right up to the highest levels.

References

1. J. M. C. DAVIDSON, '"A common system of examination at 16+": some reactions to the Schools Council Examinations Bulletin No. 23', *Modern Languages* LIV 1 (1973) 14–22.
2. B. W. PAGE, 'An alternative to 16+', *Modern Languages* LV 1 (1974) 1–5.
3. A. HARDING, B. PAGE and S. ROWELL, *Graded Objectives in Modern Languages.* London: CILT, 1980.
4. Institute of Linguists, *Syllabus of Examinations.* Available from 24a Highbury Grove, London N5 2EA.
5. English Speaking Board, *Syllabuses.* Available from 32 Roe Lane, Southport, Merseyside PR9 9EA.
6. B. BANKS, 'The Kent Mathematics Project', *The Institute of Mathematics and Its Applications* 17 (1981) 48–50.
7. M. SHAYER and P. ADEY, *Towards a Science of Science Teaching.* London: Heinemann Educational, 1981.
8. A. HARDING, B. PAGE and S. ROWELL, op. cit., pp. 2–6.
9. M. BUCKBY, P. BULL, R. FLETCHER, P. GREEN, B. PAGE and D. ROGER, *Graded Objectives and Tests for Modern Languages: an Evaluation.* London: Schools Council, 1981. Available from CILT, 20 Carlton House Terrace, London SW1Y 5AP.
10. S. BROWN, *What Do They Know? A Review of Criterion-Referenced Assessment.* Edinburgh: HMSO, 1980, p. 14.
11. ibid., p. 31.
12. A. HARDING, B. PAGE and S. ROWELL, op. cit., p. 34.
13. M. S. BYRAM, '"New objectives" in language teaching,' *Modern Languages* LIX 4 (1978) 205.
14. H. RADFORD, 'Language barriers', *Times Educational Supplement*, 8 May 1981.
15. S. A. WHITESIDE, letter to the Editor, *Times Educational Supplement*, 22 May 1981.
16. Her Majesty's Inspectorate, *Curriculum 11–16: Modern Languages. A Working Paper by the Modern Language Committee of HM Inspectorate.* London: HMSO, 1978, p. 3.

Bibliography

A RELS Examinations Trust, *A RELS Oral Examinations: Rationale, Development and Methods*. Available from A RELS, 125 High Holborn, London WC1V 6QA.

Amateur Swimming Association, *Proficiency Award Schemes*. Available from Miss L. V. Cook, 12 Kings Avenue, Woodford Green, Essex IG8 0JB.

The Associated Board of the Royal Schools of Music, *Syllabus of Music Examinations*. Available from ABRSM, 14 Bedford Square, London WC1B 3JG.

D. E. BAILEY, *A Survey of Mathematics Projects Involving Education and Employment*. Bath: Department of Mathematics, University of Bath, 1978.

B. BANKS, 'The Kent Mathematics Project', *The Institute of Mathematics and Its Applications* 17 (1981) 48–50.

R. BERGENTOFT, *Intensive Visit Organised by the British Authorities Within the Framework of the Interaction Network in the School Sector of the Modern Languages Project* (document CC-GP4(80)16). Strasbourg: Council of Europe, 1980.

D. R. BOLTON, 'York area graded language proficiency tests', *MLS* 19 (1980) 88–98.

S. BROWN, *Introducing Criterion-Referenced Assessment: Teachers' Views* (Stirling Educational Monographs No. 7). Stirling: University of Stirling, 1980.

S. BROWN, *What Do They Know? A Review of Criterion-Referenced Assessment*. Edinburgh: HMSO, 1980.

H. BRYCE, H. R. MORRISON, A. R. WILSON and I. BOFFEY, '"Eclair": a consumer report', *MLS* 20 (1980) 132–41.

M. BUCKBY, *Action!* Walton-on-Thames: Nelson, 1980.

M. BUCKBY, 'A graded system of syllabuses and examinations', *MLS* 20 (1980) 75–81.

M. BUCKBY, 'Graded objectives and tests for modern languages: an evaluation', *BJLT* 19 1 (1981) 13–14, 33.

M. BUCKBY, P. BULL, R. FLETCHER, P. GREEN, B. PAGE and D. ROGER,

Graded Objectives and Tests for Modern Languages: an Evaluation.
London: Schools Council, 1981. Available from CILT, 20 Carlton
House Terrace, London SW1Y 5AP.

J. BUGLER, 'Harsh lessons in inadequacy', *Observer*, 16 August 1981.

M. S. BYRAM, '"New objectives" in language teaching', *ML* LIX 4 (1978)
204–7.

M. S. BYRAM, 'Performance objectives and language learning', *ML* LX 2
(1979) 111–15.

B. J. CARROLL, *Testing Communicative Performance*. Oxford: Pergamon,
1980.

D. CHAPMAN, 'Graded levels of achievement in foreign-language learning
(GLAFLL)', *MLS* 19 (1980) 75–87.

J. CLARK, 'Lothian Region's levels of achievement scheme', *MLS* 15
(1978) 158–60.

J. CLARK, 'Syllabus-design for graded levels of achievement in foreign-
language learning', *MLS* 18 (1979) 25–39.

J. CLARK, 'Lothian Region's levels of achievement scheme', *MLS* 15 (1978)
foreign-language learning', *MLS* 19 (1980) 61–74.

J. L. CLARK, 'Communication in the classroom', *MLS* 21/22 (1981)
144–56.

J. CLARKE, 'Graded tests in school', *AVLJ* 17 2 (1979) 123–5.

F. COOPER, *Graded Examinations in Science* (draft). North London
Science Centre, 62–66 Highbury Grove, London N5 2AD.

S. P. CORDER, 'The teacher's contribution to the language learner's
linguistic development', *MLS* 20 (1980) 82–7.

D. COSTE, J. COURTILLON, V. FERENCZI, M. MARTINS-BALTAR, E. PAPO
and E. ROULET, *Un Niveau seuil*. Strasbourg: Council of Europe, 1976.

D. CROSS, 'A pilot investigation into the effects of a delayed start in
foreign language learning followed by an oral-based intensive course',
ML LIX 1 (1978) 82–96.

D. CROSS, 'An investigation into effects of a delayed start in main
foreign language learning', *ML* LXII 2 (1981) 85–92.

J. M. C. DAVIDSON, '"A common system of examination at 16+": some
reactions to the Schools Council Examinations Bulletin No. 23', *ML*
LIV 1 (1973) 14–22.

B. DOE, 'Step at a time language tests should replace "illogical" GCE',
TES, 13 January 1978.

P. M. R. DOIG, 'Assessment within the Modern Language Department',
MLS 20 (1980) 123–30.

P. J. DOWNES, 'Graded examinations for elementary language learners: the Oxfordshire project', *ML* LIX 3 (1978) 153–6.

The Duke of Edinburgh's Award, *Annual Report 1980*. Available from DEA, 5 Prince of Wales Terrace, Kensington, London W8 5PG.

English Speaking Board, *Syllabuses*. Available from ESB, 32 Roe Lane, Southport, Merseyside PR9 9EA.

A. FITZGERALD, 'Corridor of power', *Mathematics in School* 7 1 (1977) 23–5.

The Football Association, *Superskills Awards*. Available from FA, 16 Lancaster Gate, London W2 3LW.

E. GARNER, 'Going for GOALS', *TES*, 6 February 1981.

K. L. GORDON, 'Oxfordshire Modern Languages Achievement Certificate (OMLAC)' *MLS* 19 (1980) 99–114.

Graded French Tests. Walton-on-Thames: Nelson, 1980.

Guildhall School of Music and Drama, *Grade Examinations Syllabuses*. Available from GSMD, Barbican, London EC2Y 8DT.

A. HARDING and J. A. NAYLOR, 'Graded objectives in second language learning: a way ahead', *AVLJ* 17 3 (1979) 169–74.

A. HARDING and B. PAGE, 'An alternative model for modern language examinations', *AVLJ* 12 3 (1974) 237–41.

A. HARDING, B. PAGE and S. ROWELL, *Graded Objectives in Modern Languages*. London: CILT, 1980.

D. HARRIS, review of 'Eclair', *MLS* 19 (1980) 130–36.

A. HARRISON, 'Incline of difficulty in French: an experiment in test setting', *AVLJ* 15 2 (1977) 135–46.

A. HARRISON, 'Test development: theory and practice', *Bulletin Pédagogique IUT* 51 (1977) 19–32.

A. HARRISON, *Techniques for Evaluating a Learner's Ability to Apply Threshold Level Proficiency to Everyday Communication* (document DECS/EES(79)77). Strasbourg: Council of Europe, 1979.

A. HARRISON, 'Current views on the Institute's examinations: extracts from the Examination Review report', *The Incorporated Linguist* 19 2 (1980) 38–42.

E. W. HAWKINS, *Modern Languages in the Curriculum*. Cambridge: CUP, 1981.

Headmasters' Conference, *The Teaching of Modern Languages: a View for the 1980s* (HMC Modern Languages Report No. 2). London: HMC, 1980.

Her Majesty's Inspectorate, *Curriculum 11–16: Modern Languages. A*

55

Working Paper by the Modern Language Committee of H M Inspectorate.
London: HMSO, 1978.

The Hockey Association, *Rose Award Scheme.* Available from
J. F. Cadman, The Red House, Great Horkesley, Colchester, Essex
CO6 4HA.

ILEA, *Eclair.* Warwick: Mary Glasgow Publications, 1980.

The Institute of Linguists, *Syllabus of Examinations.* Available from IL,
24a Highbury Grove, London N5 2EA.

International Dance Teachers' Association, *Theatre Dance Syllabus – Set
Work – Glossaries.* Available from IDTA, 76 Bennett Road, Brighton
BN2 5JL.

D. JOHNSON, 'ILEA graded tests working party: a progess report', *MLS*
19 (1980) 115–21.

R. JOHNSTONE, 'An interim outline of the "Tour de France" syllabus for
first-year classes', *MLS* 19 (1980) 34–50.

T. C. JUPP and S. HODLIN, *Industrial English.* London: Heinemann
Educational, 1975.

The London Academy of Music and Dramatic Art, *Examination Syllabuses.*
Available from LAMDA, Tower House, 226 Cromwell Road,
London SW5 OSR.

P. MCKENZIE, 'Producing and teaching a school-based non-certificate
French course with a language core', *MLS* 18 (1979) 64–75.

B. G. MARTIN, 'Teaching "Eclair" in Dunbarton Division', *MLS* 18 (1979)
39–44.

Modern Language Association, 'Submission by the MLA to the Parliamentary
Select Committee on Education, Science and the Arts in
connection with an inquiry into the Secondary School Curriculum and
Examinations: February 1981', *ML* LXII 2 (1981) 102–9.

P. D. MORRIS, 'Children's attitude to French at 13+', *ML* LIX 4 (1978)
177–83.

H. R. MORRISON, 'Pupil profiles', *MLS* 20 (1980) 113–22.

K. MORROW, *Techniques of Evaluation for a Notional Syllabus.* London:
RSA, 1977. Available from the Royal Society of Arts, 18 John Adam
Street, London WC2N 6EZ.

K. MORROW, 'Communicative language testing: revolution or evolution?',
in C. J. Brumfit and K. Johnson (eds.), *The Communicative Approach
to Language Teaching.* Oxford: OUP, 1979.

A. MOYS, A. HARDING, B. PAGE and V. J. PRINTON, *Modern Language
Examinations at Sixteen-plus: a Critical Analysis.* London: CILT, 1980.

North West Regional Examinations Board, *English as a Second Language: Notes for the Guidance of Teachers*. Manchester: NWREB, 1980. Available from the North West Regional Examinations Board, Orbit House, Albert Street, Eccles, Manchester M30 OWL.

J. W. OLLER, *Language Tests at School*. Harlow: Longman, 1979.

OMLAC, *New Objectives in Modern Language Teaching: Defined Syllabuses and Tests in French and German*. Dunton Green, Sevenoaks: Hodder & Stoughton, 1978.

OMLAC, *New Objectives in Modern Language Teaching, Book 2*. Dunton Green, Sevenoaks: Hodder & Stoughton, 1981.

M. OSKARSSON, *Self-assessment in Foreign Language Learning*. Oxford: Pergamon, 1980.

B. PAGE, 'An alternative to 16+', *ML* LV 1 (1974) 1–5.

B. PAGE, 'Graded examinations', *ML* LIX 1 (1978) 97–101.

B. PARKINSON, R. MITCHELL and R. JOHNSTONE, *Mastery Learning in Foreign Language Teaching: a Case Study* (Stirling Educational Monographs No. 8). Stirling: University of Stirling, 1981.

A. PECK, 'Communicative methodology and its implications for teaching strategy', *ML* LX 3 (1979) 127–36.

G. PERREN, ' "Levels of Performance" in foreign languages', in Emmans *et al.*, *The Use of Foreign Languages in the Private Sector of Industry and Commerce*. York: Language Teaching Centre, 1974.

A. E. G. PILLINER, 'Norm-referenced and criterion-referenced tests – an evaluation', in *Issues in Educational Assessment*. Edinburgh: HMSO, 1979.

Pitman Examinations Institute, *Regulations and Syllabuses*. Available from PEI, Godalming, Surrey GU7 1UU.

RSA, *Examinations in the Communicative Use of English as a Foreign Language: Specifications and Specimen Papers*. London: RSA, n.d.

RSA, *Modern Languages: Preliminary Level Examination Explanatory Booklet* (draft).

H. RADFORD, 'Language barriers', *TES*, 8 May 1981.

A. REID, 'A report on the use of "Tour de France"', *MLS* 20 (1980) 46–52.

Report from the York area working party on language proficiency tests, *ML* LIX 3 (1978) 150–52.

I. F. ROOS-WIJGH, 'Testing speaking proficiency through functional dialogues', in J. L. D. Clark (ed.), *Direct Teaching of Speaking Proficiency: Theory and Application*. Princeton, NJ: Educational Testing Service, 1978.

M. SHAYER and P. ADEY, *Towards a Science of Science Teaching*. London: Heinemann Educational, 1981.

R. SULLIVAN, letter to the Editor, *TES*, 22 May 1981.

J. L. M. TRIM, *Developing a Unit/Credit Scheme of Adult Language Learning*. Oxford: Pergamon, 1980.

Trinity College of Music, London, *Syllabuses of Grade and Diploma Examinations*. Available from TCM, Mandeville Place, London W1M 6AQ.

R. M. VALETTE, 'Using classroom tests to improve instruction', *AVLJ* 12 3 (1974) 217–21.

R. M. VALETTE, *Modern Language Testing: a Handbook*. New York: Harcourt Brace Jovanovich, 1977.

J. A. VAN EK, *The Threshold Level for Modern Language Learning in Schools*. Harlow: Longman, 1977.

M. WHALLEY and S. WHITESIDE, 'Graded tests in French and German', *Essex Education* 34 2 (1980) 37–8.

S. A. WHITESIDE, letter to the Editor, *TES*, 22 May 1981.

D. WRIGHT, *How Much? How Many?* Sunbury-on-Thames: Nelson, 1980.

Journals:

AVLJ:	*Audio-Visual Language Journal*
BJLT:	*The British Journal of Language Teaching*
ML:	*Modern Languages*
MLS:	*Modern Languages in Scotland*
TES:	*Times Educational Supplement*

Appendices

Table 1 Starting dates

		1975	76	77	78	79	80	(81)	(82)	(83)	n.a
French:	group formed	1	1	7	14	7	5				2
	teaching started	1	2	1	12	14	2	4			1
	tests first taken	1		2	3	12	12	4	1	1	1
German:	group formed	1		4	8	3	4				1
	teaching started		1	1	8	5	4				2
	tests first taken	1		1	2	7	6	2			2
Spanish:	group formed	1		2	3	3	2				
	teaching started		1		4	4	2				
	tests first taken		1	1	2	4	2				1

Table 2 Numbers of candidates

1980 Levels	1	2	3	4	5	Year totals
F	50427	13696	1432	220	3	65778
G	4580	883				5463
S	381					381
R						

Totals by language

F	187974
G	22342
S	1531
R	115

1981 (estimated)

	1	2	3	4	5	Year totals
F	80954	35249	5250	740	3	122196
G	12213	3940	726			16879
S	1020	130				1150
R			115			115

Table 3 Size of groups, French

N cands	1980 Levels					1981				
	1	2	3	4	5	1	2	3	4	5
200	4	2	3	2	1	1	1	5	3	1
200–500	4	5	2			3	6	3	1	
501–1000	7	4	1			5	4	4		
1000–3000	7	3				10	6			
3000	6	1				8	4			

Table 4 Size of groups, German and Spanish

German	1980 Levels		1981			Spanish	1980		1981	
N cands	1	2	1	2	3		1	2	1	2
200	2	2	2	3	1		4		3	2
201–500	2	2	3	6						
501–1000	3		3		1				1	
1000	1		3	1						

Table 5 Levels and years, French

How many years on average have the candidates been learning the language when they take the tests at each level?

Years	Levels				
	1	2	3	4	5
1	8	1			
1	1				
1½	1				
1–2	3				
1–3	1	1	1		
1–4	1				
2	8	4	1		
2½		2			
2			1		
2–3	5	4		1	
2–4		1	1		

Years	Levels				
	1	2	3	4	5
3	3	11	3		
3+			1		
3½			1		
3–4				1	1
4			2	1	1
4–5			1		
5				1	2

Table 6 Pupils not awarded certificates

What usually happens to those who are not awarded a certificate?

same class, remedial out of class	6
same class, remedial in class	7
another class	5
same class, keep going	3
no fixed procedure	6
n.a.	10

Table 7 Availability of syllabus, French

To whom is the syllabus or statement of objectives available?

teachers	36
pupils	13
parents	6
general public	6
anyone (published as book)	2

Table 8 Origin of syllabuses

	F	G	S
own	23	15	6
developed by another group	5	5	2
adapted from another group	8	2	2

Table 9 Origin of tests

	F	G	S
own	30	15	7
developed by another group	3	3	
adapted from another group	5	2	3

Table 10 Groups taught on syllabus

	F	G	S
a under 16, lower ability	17	6	4
b under 16, all abilities	31	18	9
6th form	6	5	4
adults	13	10	4

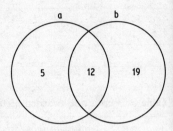

Table 11 Groups tests intended for

	F	G	S
a under 16, lower ability	15	6	5
b under 16, all abilities	30	18	9
6th form	3	3	2
adults	9	9	5

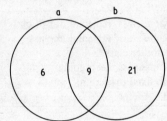

Table 12 Groups tested

	F	G	S
a under 16, lower ability	15	5	4
b under 16, all abilities	26	16	7
6th form	4	3	2
adults	9	8	3

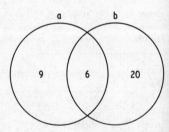

Table 13 Syllabus descriptions, French

Are your tests related to any explicit syllabus/statement of objectives or level of performance?

	own	others'	unspec.	
yes	34	19	7	8
no	3			

64

Table 14 Definition of syllabus

If you have an explicit syllabus or statement of objectives, how is it defined?

			Clusters:		1 each:
a	structural	8	a–f	4	abce
b	functional	20	bcd	4	abcde
c	notional	19	bc	3	ad
d	situational	28	bcde	3	ade
e	lexical	15	d	3	bdef
f	the 'four skills'	14	df	3	bdf
g	background	1	bcdf	2	cd
			def	2	de
					e
					f

Table 15 Component titles, French

What components are separately assessed at each level?

Skills		Activities	
listening, listening comprehension	34	role playing	1
aural, aural comprehension	2	conversation	1
speaking	31	talking	1
oral	3	essay	1
reading, reading comprehension	26	correspondence	1
survival reading	1	sequence	1
extensive reading	1		
written comprehension	3	*Unclassified*	
writing	12	background	2
limited writing	1	orientation	1
listening/reading	3	written paper	1
writing/reading	2	comprehension	1
listening/speaking	1	continuous assessment	1
		the assessment is criterion-referenced	1

Table 16 Mark allocations, French

Please indicate the percentage of the overall mark allocated to each component.

Level 1, N = 24	Listening	Speaking	Reading	Background*
Average	36	30	32	17
Range	20–50	24–40	20–45	10–23

Level 2, N = 21	Listening	Speaking	Reading	Background*
Average	36	29	33	17
Range	15–50	20–40	20–40	10–23

Level 3, N = 12	Listening	Speaking	Reading	Writing†
Average	34	30	28	15
Range	22–67	20–40	22–40	10–29

Level 4, N = 5	Listening	Speaking	Reading	Writing
Average	26	33	24	15
Range	20–30	30–40	15–30	5–20

*N = 2 | †N = 5

Table 17 Use of certificates

For what audience is the certificate intended?		What steps are taken to inform people outside the school of the significance of the certificate?	
pupils	36	certificate explains itself	8
others in school	13	parents' evenings, info sheets	6
parents	26	local newspaper	3
outside users	11	careers service	3
		misc.	9
		none	15

Table 18 Endorsement of certificates

Who gives the official endorsement to the scheme?	
a school	8
b LEA	29
c other	5

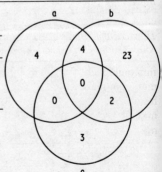

66

Table 19 Test components in certificates

Are attainments in different test components reported separately on the certificate?	Is any other form of profile reporting used?
yes 6	yes 5
no 29	no 29
n.a. 2	n.a. 3

Table 20 Meaning of certificate

What information is given on the certificate about the syllabus?		What information is given on the certificate about the candidate's achievement?	
a none	8	**a** none	8
b skills	21	**b** skills	14
c activities	22	**c** activities	23
d other	2	**d** other	6

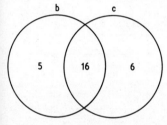
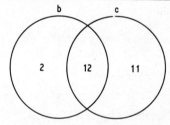

Table 21 Grading

What form does the overall grading take at each level?		How is the overall pass grade determined?	
pass/fail	20	overall mark	27
credit/pass/fail	14	fixed pass rate	9
more than three	3		

How are the marks in the different test components combined into an overall 'pass' grade?	
minimum sum	29
minimum mark	2
hurdles	3
misc.	3
n.a.	4

Table 22 Successes

N responses = 96; points mentioned = 27

Pupils
motivation/enthusiasm (32)
increase in take-up (14)
sense of achievement
'It works!'

Teachers
rethinking teaching (19)
motivation/enthusiasm (7)
better rewards
more relaxed teaching
working together
self-assessment
wanting to teach less able
contact with other teachers
in-service value
expertise extended
education students working with teachers

Methods
precision in teaching (2)
communicative methodology
re-emphasizing oral work
long-term change of method
European studies abandoned

Organization
school take-up
more and more want to join
persuading others to join
cooperation between schools
overspill into other subjects

parent enthusiasm

too early to say

Table 23 Distinctive features of groups

N responses = 65; points mentioned = 51

Teachers
involvement (3)
own teaching materials (2)
large number involved
in-service value
rethinking of criteria
voluntary meetings
growing test expertise
no travel expenses claimed
continuity *and* fresh thinking
enthusiasm for the scheme
discussion of what to expect
pooling of ideas helpful

Test content
skills separately assessed (2)
mode distinction
own syllabus
non-derivative
more oral work
massive speaking, little writing
defined content: functions
impetus of materials
efficient production of successful tests
pair work in tests

Organization
collective (3)
large size of operation (3)
cooperative venture (2)
wide area/many schools involved (2)
with college of education (2)
individual school initiative
school-based work
all schools in area
three schools together
two boroughs together
Tuesday afternoons free for it
$1\frac{1}{2}$ full-time employees on it
involvement of teacher trainees
support of LEA and outside experts

Assessments
continuous assessment
individual credits
profiling
progress cards
standard across borough

Misc.
EEC grant
foundation course
syllabus then materials then test
group + any teacher

not distinctive (3)

Pupils
lower ability groups (2)
includes adults
for *all* learners
needs with German families
visits of German children to school

Table 24 Problems

N responses = 63; points mentioned = 25

Administration
secretarial help (10)
extra work/load/time (9)
lack of LEA/other support (4)
communications (3)
distribution of materials (3)
duplicating (2)
administrative constraints (2)
finance/future finance by LEA (2)
finding time for meetings (2)
travelling to meetings
production of certificate
expansion in numbers
widespread county
release for minor language teachers

Teachers
conservatism (2)
coming to agreed philosophy
same small band
stability of group

Tests
organizing orals (10)
classroom management
maintaining standards
validating with small numbers
pre-testing
scarcity of published materials
production of own materials

69

Table 25 Ideal assessment

N responses = 45; points mentioned = 12

Applications	Systems
in action in France, Germany ... (24)	self-evaluation (4)
mock France, Germany ... (4)	profiling (2)
controlled situations abroad	smaller, more frequent assessments
L2 people in England	on-going assessment
	group testing
	monitored by outsiders (e.g. ed. students)
	not an ideal world (4)
	'We haven't discussed this.'

Appendix B   Comments on GOML

The following quotations have been taken somewhat at random from various sources: replies to the questionnaire, local authority newsletters, articles and letters in the press. They give some indication of the range of personal views expressed by those involved in GOML and by those outside.

'The gap between the pretentious rhetoric of theorists leading yet another crusade and the stern reality of the classroom is notoriously wide. Objectives such as "communicative competence" glibly applied to the rudimentary and desultory instruction – *saupoudrage horaire* – in modern languages offered in most secondary schools, are just empty slogans ... Whatever new syllabuses and tests emerge, foreign languages will continue to be the sick man of the comprehensive curriculum until steps are taken to reinforce (and refresh through in-service provision) the small band of highly competent teachers who at present keep the subject alive (and every "working party", as a possible escape from drudgery, tends to reduce their number).'

'Functional/notional syllabuses, differentiated aims, threshold level, communicative competence – he dismisses these terms as mere catch-phrases. May I suggest that he and his students should sit down and rethink a foreign language syllabus in precisely these terms, and that they carry their thinking through to the 16 + age level and beyond, where the real language barriers that exist are those set up by outmoded assessment procedures. All is not gloom on the modern language front. There are many teachers who spend many hours in working groups, not in order to escape from drudgery, as he suggests, but in order to re-establish foreign languages as a viable subject on the comprehensive school curriculum.'

'What is certain is that a good attack on the language and a sense of achievement are indispensable foundations for a useful apprenticeship. For this reason the unit/credit and graded test movement must be seen, among some disappointments encountered by language teachers in the 1970s, as a promising approach to reducing and defining the learning load, while motivating the learner, especially the young and less able learner.'

'... [tests designed for pupils of lower ability] was our original intention but so many of [all abilities] have become interested and wish to take part. Teachers have referred to better motivation/more appropriate objectives, etc., and included a wider range of pupils accordingly.'

'... we feel *strongly* the scheme is for all and not just average and less able.'

'It has sprung from a desire within the County to redefine objectives for middle- and lower-ability candidates.'

'We thought originally that the test as such was less important than the defined syllabus and the way in which the syllabus was taught. We therefore set out to produce appropriate teaching materials as our first aim. In fact we didn't look at the test at all until just before we used it.'

'In all some twenty-five teachers were involved. The time needed to deal with each detail was phenomenal, but the in-service value has been inestimable. As well as drawing up a description of syllabus content and producing teaching materials, teachers have scrutinized existing published materials, shared ideas on teaching methods and become aware of the extreme care needed in the writing of valid test-items.'

'Impressed by the concern that language teachers demonstrate for their pupils. Discussions long and often heated – sense of involvement in something that is very worthwhile.'

'... [greatest problems were] slowness of timid or over-conservative colleagues to join in this new approach to language assessment and teaching.'

'Have my attitudes changed? I think so. I'm much less worried by inaccuracy in written work. Communication has become more important – this has been a traumatic experience for one brought up to worship at the altar of the complete sentence.'

'With the stress being shifted from grammatical accuracy in meaningless exercises to communicative ability in relevant situations even pupils who were receiving remedial help in their own language discovered that they could accomplish simple tasks in the foreign language.'

'Motivation is the key. They want to keep up to date with their system jotters and like to progress through their progress cards and they really enjoy the paired conversations.'

'The course in German that we took was very helpful. It showed us how to cope in certain situations, which would be very useful if we got lost in Germany, or had to buy something vital.'

'By the end we had all passed grade 1. I think this is an excellent method of teaching a language, and I would recommend it to anyone.'

'... I was amused and impressed at the way in which a day trip to France validated the criteria by which you selected the material included in level 1. Our 13-year-olds really could cope. Walking down the main shopping street was like a repetition of a recent lesson and it was quite a thrill to watch two not very gifted linguists sit down with complete confidence in a café and order and pay for their drinks – not a moment's hesitation on their part, nor the waiter's.'

'... [greatest successes included] pupils coming back from France saying "It works!"'

'An ideal world in which language assessment and certification is not vested in entrenched power-groups with careers to make and axes to grind, irrespective of the real needs of pupils, is in itself so unlikely that the question has no meaning.'

'Face to face with native speakers in the target country [would be ideal] but it is not altogether realistic. Learning to communicate in a foreign language is only part of the school-based foreign language programme. I am more impressed by the normally uncooperative fourth-year drop-outs who actually thank their French teacher for a good lesson, than by their results in a test. They may never come face to face with a native speaker, but they are obviously convinced that a foreign language is not an imposed irrelevance in their lives. Hopefully, they will take this favourable attitude with them when they leave school.'

Appendix C Test schemes in mathematics: some examples

1 Hertfordshire Mathematics Achievement Certificate

'The Certificate provides a means of listing those areas of mathematics in which a particular pupil has achieved success during the latter part of the secondary-school course. Although the range of topics so recorded will usually be narrower than that which would lead to an award in a public examination, their specification in this manner has been found to be of great value both to Careers Advisory Staff and Industrial Selection and Training Staff. The award of an Achievement Certificate is dependent on the pupil producing a high standard of work in general mathematics and demonstrating mastery within a carefully defined range of calculations.

'The scheme is working successfully in our all-ability schools since it provides (a) a basis for a relevant course for non-academic pupils; (b) a set of realistic targets for pupils; (c) a positive statement individual to each pupil which details areas of achievement; (d) an effective incentive device since entries on Certificates are cumulative.'

Contact: R. W. Shaw, County Adviser for Mathematics, Hertfordshire County Council Education Department, County Hall, Hertford SG13 8DF.

2 Huntingdon and Peterborough Number Index Test

'In essence, the test is designed to be a guide for employers as to the "arithmetic" ability of 16-year-old secondary-school pupils ... The test consists of forty questions to be answered in thirty minutes. The questions are based around eight topic headings: (1) Mental Arithmetic; (2) Four Arithmetic Operations; (3) Length ... Every question used has been extensively pre-tested in local schools and categorized, on the basis of the pre-test results, according to its degree of difficulty. This enables us to ensure that the final paper contains questions appropriate to a wide range of abilities. The test is given, under exam conditions, to all fifth-year pupils in all local secondary schools on the same day in November ... The grades, ranging from A to J, indicate the decile into which the pupil falls ... The test has now been in operation for three years (1978, 1979, 1980) and has, so far, been well received both by employers and schools.'

Contact: I. M. Repper, Head of Maths/Science Faculty, Saint Paul's School, York Road, Peterborough PE1 3BP.

74

3 *Judgemeadow: Joint Schools Numeracy Profile*

'... its aims are: (1) To produce a record for the employer of a child's ability in mathematics; (2) To encourage a pupil to improve his/her standard in mathematics; (3) To act as a diagnostic tool for the teacher by indicating pupils' weaknesses. The syllabus contains five areas of work, namely Arithmetic, Money, Measurement, Home Mathematics and Further Mathematics. Each of these main categories are then broken down into smaller topics for testing purposes ... A pupil's ability in each of these topic areas is assessed by a test containing ten questions, which are marked on a right or wrong basis ... The children are told they have "passed" if they score 9 or 10 out of 10 ... The children take these tests throughout their fifth year, and there is no theoretical limit to the number of retakes a child is allowed. All the results, failures as well as successes, including the dates on which they were taken, are marked on a record card, and it is this record card that forms the "profile" or final certificate. For the employer's ease, the front of the record card contains a bar chart showing the child's best score on each topic area ... (1) Children have more obvious and attainable goals ... (2) Very easy to grade ... gives better motivation as many children at this level require quick rewards and not long term goals. (3) Each question tests a specific skill so if a child gets a question wrong the teacher has an idea of what areas a child needs teaching in ... (4) Children can repeat test items, which gives them the sense of improvement ... (5) Children have a course which lasts the whole year ... (6) An employer can see at a glance which topics a pupil is good at and which bad ... (7) As the profile is being built up with every test a child takes, an employer can ask to see it at any stage of the course from Christmas to the end of the school year ... (8) It gives the employer a chance to influence the child's mathematics in the last year, as he can specify topics which the child should pass in before applying for employment. (9) It is unlikely that an employer will require these children to master all the skills at once. It is more likely that he will require complete mastery of a particular skill, these tests help by encouraging children to improve their standards by repeating tests and improving their results.'

Contact: H. W. Pettman, Head of Mathematics, Judgemeadow Community College, Marydene Drive, Evington, Leicester LE5 6HP.

4 *Kent Mathematics Project*

'The KMP is a material bank from which teachers can select appropriate courses for their pupils. The material bank extends over nine levels, and is arranged in a conceptual hierarchy which has evolved over the fourteen years of classroom use. Level 1 contains material dealing with concepts believed to be suitable for average 9-year-olds, while levels 7, 8 and 9 contain material suitable for O-level candidates.'
'... all pupils working at their own personal ability levels is probably the most

powerful ingredient in maintaining their interest. The KMP system ensures that each pupil is operating at his or her own level with material which challenges but is mastered. Children work on a bundle of about ten tasks which, when completed, are tested. If the converted test mark is, say, 70 per cent, the teacher investigates the 30 per cent loss and clears up mistakes and misunderstandings. The pupil then receives a second mark approaching 100 per cent and during this vital part of the scheme the teacher has gained information about the pupil's needs in terms of additional work on a topic, readiness for the next stage with possible looping forward, and what topics to pursue ... Because all learning is consolidated before advance, each pupil operates in a personal mathematics learning world which is always successful.'

Contact: B. Banks, The West Kent Teachers' Centre, Deacon Court, Culverden Park Road, Tunbridge Wells, Kent, TN4 9QX.

5 *Norton: Basic Numeracy Scheme*

'The essence of the scheme is that five or ten minutes of each maths session is devoted to doing basic numeracy work from a series of booklets, either a mechanical practice set, a simple "everyday" maths problem or a set of mental questions. After a while, with plenty of repetition, most pupils begin to enjoy the exercise, mainly because they are successful and the exercises are not long enough to become a bore. Pupils of all abilities in the third, fourth and fifth years follow the scheme ... At the end of the third year the whole year takes an examination in mental, mechanical and problem-solving ability. A high standard of accuracy is required (about 70 per cent pass mark) and method marks are allowed only in the problem-solving section of the paper. A certificate is awarded to successful candidates and the exam is retaken in the fourth and fifth years when endorsements to the certificate can be gained ...

'(1) Goals must be set which are *seen* to be attainable by *every* pupil, given, of course, the necessary effort. (2) Rewards, usually in terms of success, must be achieved at an early stage (especially by lower-ability pupils) in order to maintain and increase motivation. In my scheme many pupils' sets should be marked immediately by the teacher and gaining full marks on a set of five mechanical questions is an early success enjoyed by most pupils – they can measure their own performance and progress. The larger success in the form of a printed certificate comes towards the end of the year. (Note there are no grades or different levels in the scheme – everyone either passes or fails.) (3) Much of the material is relevant to the pupil and/or recognized by him/her to be essential learning material which "everybody should know". (4) Paramount is the enthusiasm and commitment of the teacher – any scheme stands or falls by this one factor.'

Contact: D. Wright, Head of Maths Department, Norton School, Langton Road, Norton, Malton, North Yorks.

6 *Redditch: CSE Mode III*

'... in conjunction with the Abbey High School, Redditch, we considered the Mode I mathematics syllabus offered by the West Midlands Examinations Board, accepted its contents as being sufficient to prove a good mathematics knowledge for the majority of candidates, and constructed a Mode III scheme around it.

'This necessitated the Mode I syllabus being divided into sections, each section being made up of topics understandable to a specific ability level. These sections were numbered after the CSE grades. They were designed to represent grades 1, 2, 3, 4 and 5. Each of these grades was "self-contained" and had its own examination paper which tested its contents. Thus, we had created a choice of five papers for a candidate to take which depended on his ability, rather than one paper to suit all levels of competence. The paper which the candidate would take would be decided in consultation with his classteacher, and would be based on topics within his capabilities which should not "out-face" him. Each examination would consist of two papers, each of two hours and would be of the pass/fail type with the pass mark at approximately 50 per cent.

'As we were then in a position to examine specific levels of attainment, we next considered the possibility of testing each candidate at regular intervals during his fourth and fifth years using papers designed to test his attainment and to provide him with an incentive to strive for a higher grade each time. Finally it was decided to test on three occasions; summer of the fourth year, Christmas of the fifth year and the summer of the fifth year ...

'By taking these successive examinations from the end of the fourth year, each candidate is able to see, and hopefully learn, from the first two examinations taken but not, I hasten to add, the final paper. This allows him to appreciate where his mistakes were made, etc., and to use the information gained usefully.'

Contact: P. S. Whiteoak, Head of Mathematics, The Leys High School, Woodrow Drive, Redditch B98 7UH.

7 *SLAPONS (School Leaver's Attainment Profile of Numerical Skills)*

'... a test of attainment in numerical skills, to be done in any of the months November, December, January or February by pupils in their last year of compulsory schooling ... so that the results would be available at interviews for employers ... the result should be presented in the form of an individual attainment profile ... schools should be encouraged to run the test, at approximately the same time of year, for their fourth year ... employers should be presented with a copy of the test so that they can identify which items are relevant to their requirements ... employers should be invited, primarily for their own convenience, to draw up transparent templates of the job requirements to superimpose over the applicant's profile at interview ... employers might be asked to show their templates to schoolteachers and be happy to explain their choice.'

Content: natural (whole) numbers, fractions, decimals, related thinking, approximations, estimations. Add, subtract, multiply, divide for each of the first three of these; conversions F to D, D to F and F to %.

Contact: R. L. Lindsay, Lecturer, Shell Centre for Mathematical Education, The University, Nottingham, NG7 2RD.

8 *Wiltshire: Assessment Materials for Mathematics in Schools*

'The aim of this project was for teachers and advisers in seven of the South-West Counties to produce assessment materials in mathematics for use by teachers in the classroom. These would help in the measurement of progress, and the diagnosis of learning difficulties of individual children ... The project in Wiltshire set out to establish test items for each topic in the Wiltshire Guidelines in Mathematics 5–13 Years ... The assessment materials are an aid for you in the classroom: to help you to help children; to help you find out how children are progressing, and any difficulties they are experiencing; to amplify the intention of the Guidelines for you; to provide you with some objective information, in a convenient form, which will complement your own observations about children ... There are two kinds of cards: those written in Italic script are intended for you to use in an oral and/or practical situation. Most of these are for use with younger children; those printed in Roman script are intended for pupils to work from directly, on paper or in an exercise book, just as they would from a teaching work card ... For practical purposes the cards have been packaged at four levels. These follow the sequential development which is indicated in the Guidelines ... They should be used informally, as part of your normal classroom practice, as an integral part of the learning process. In general, you will use these assessments at the end of a stage of learning so that you can plan the next stage. You should be reasonably confident that any child who is given a card will succeed with the majority of its content. Similarly, the children themselves should feel confident and secure when they meet them ... There are no marking systems, and no "pass" or "fail" gradings. It is for you to make a judgement about the readiness of the child to proceed to the next stage of work, or whether a further period of consolidation on certain aspects is required.'

Contact: Anita Straker, County Mathematics Adviser, Wiltshire County Council, Education Department, County Hall, Trowbridge BA14 8JB.

78

Appendix D   From the report of a meeting on 'Grading GOML levels 3, 4, 5 and 6'

The meeting was held at the Albert Mansbridge Centre, Leeds, on 5–7 June 1981.
The following are the recommendations of Working Party 2, whose brief was to
make recommendations for the relationship between GOML tests and the proposed
new system of public examinations. They are reproduced from GOML Newsletter
No. 5, August 1981, compiled by Sheila Rowell, CILT, 20 Carlton House Terrace,
London SW1Y 5AP, for the GOML Coordinating Committee.

1

The group believes that the ideals embodied in GOML can be attained through
the public examination system if the will exists to provide an appropriate framework. Such a framework could emerge as a result of comparatively minor adjust-
ments, mainly in terminology, on the part of the GOML groups on the one hand
and the 16+ working parties on the other.

2   *GOML levels*

Because there are so many local GOML schemes there is no commonly recognized
scale of the levels. A candidate's performance deemed at level 3 by one group
may be deemed level 4 by another. This is not through a deep-seated difference
about absolute standards but merely through a difference of calibration on a
scale. If GOML is to be seen as a nationally recognized assessment system, groups
will have to arrive at an agreed scale of levels.

3   *The new public examination grades*

The proposed new public examination will lead to an award of seven pass grades
replacing (though it is not clear whether they are to be strictly equivalent to) the
existing GCE O-level grades A, B, C and the CSE grades 2, 3, 4, 5. An obvious
step for GOML in achieving a rapprochement with 16+ is to divide its scale
into seven levels. This would mean redistribution of the present levels of most
schemes (which tend to envisage only four or five stages to O-level), but this
should be easily attainable given the resourcefulness and spirit of cooperation
within the movement. We would then have two parallel grading systems, thus

16+ grades:	7	6	5	4	3	2	1
GOML levels:	1	2	3	4	5	6	7

The last two would correspond to the expected performance of a high-ability 16-year-old after five years' secondary-school language study.

The suggested grading system for the new public examination perpetuates one of the many negative aspects of the present examinations: the bottom grade (7) is seen as a failure to reach the highest grade (1). By the simple method of reversing the order of the numbers, attitudes to the examination might begin to change. Grade 1 (the lowest grade) could be seen as a first successful step in language learning leading to other grades above it. These grades could then correspond to the GOML levels and represent the same levels of competence. By numbering in this manner we would have an open-ended system which could proceed smoothly from the needs of secondary school students to those of students in tertiary and higher education.

16+ grades:	1	2	3	4	5	6	7
GOML levels:	1	2	3	4	5	6	7

The last two would correspond to the expected performance of a high-ability 16-year-old after five years' secondary-school language study.

Thus a smooth transition could be made to levels beyond the present O-level/CSE.

4 Age group

The new examination, like the present O level, must be available to all age groups and therefore it must not be seen as tied to the school leaving age of 16+. If, because of possible confusion, the present title General Certificate of Education cannot be used, then some equally neutral title must be found. The principle that the candidate could enter the examination at any age at any level would be another common feature of the GOML scheme and the new GCE.

5 Graded tests as a national examination system

The sole practical requirement of this development is to have a *series* of tests, each corresponding to a *level*: tests which already exist in prototype in a number of GOML schemes up to CSE level and which are likely to reach O-level equivalent in the foreseeable future. It would be inappropriate and over-expensive for pupils to take each of these seven official grades. In practice pupils in secondary schools would enter for an official examination only at the end of their language study *whenever that might occur in their school course*. Teachers would also normally

80

administer informal examinations possibly based on the official grade definitions and possibly locally certificated as in many GOML schemes at the moment. These would serve as a reliable guide to pupils and teachers about which of the official grades to enter for.

6 Ability range

The new examination working parties have found it very difficult to solve the problem posed by the need to cater for a wider ability range within one examination. Some talk of an 'extension paper' which many will claim merely perpetuates the O-level/CSE division the new examination should seek to replace. Adapting the GOML system, which is already well tried, would seem to us to provide an acceptable solution.

7 Some possible objections countered

a   It might seem that a public examination system based on seven separate sets of tests would be impossibly complex and expensive. We would reply that, for several years now, volunteer groups of teachers working in their spare time, with, as a rule, virtually no funds whatsoever, have found it possible to produce tests of the envisaged type at up to four levels so far.

b   GOML groups might feel that they would be handing over control of all their level tests to the Examination Board. Two things should be remembered, however:

i the Mode III system should still exist (this may have to be fought for);
ii GOML systems will in any case have to reflect the requirements of public examinations if they are to exist at all beyond being low-level, non-recognized examinations for the low achiever.

8 Other subjects

As modern linguists we are well aware of the difficulty of 'going it alone' (with the GOML approach). Yet it is our belief that we do not need to be alone. Ours are not the only subjects in which there is a notion of *progression*. We would maintain that whenever such a notion is tenable the GOML approach is applicable. Mathematics teachers are embarking on various graded schemes and others, if encouraged, may follow.

9

It is thirty years since our examination system was last extensively revised. It can hardly be said that on that occasion it was brought up to date in any serious sense.

Today we risk facing another set of untidy compromises and reshuffles which will again create a system which is out of date before it is implemented. We are not calling for 'pie in the sky' idealism, but for the adoption of ideas which have undergone considerable scrutiny and such practical testing as has been possible. We believe that the recommendations made above combine a simplicity of principle with considerable benefits for teacher effectiveness and student motivation.

Members of the Monitoring and Review Group

A. H. Jennings (*Chair*)	Formerly Headmaster, Ecclesfield School, Sheffield
R. Aitken	Director of Education, Coventry
B. Arthur	HM Inspectorate of Schools
J. J. Billington	Deputy Headmaster, High Pavement Sixth Form College, Nottingham
D. Foster	Churchill School, Bristol
J. Hedger	Department of Education and Science
P. Herbert	The Elliott School, London SW15
D. I. Morgan	W. R. Tuson College, Preston, Lancashire
R. Potts	Harraby School, Carlisle
J. Symonds	Southern Universities' Joint Board

Schools Council staff

L. Orr	Principal Research Officer

Other publications from the Schools Council

Graded objectives and tests for modern languages: an evaluation
by Michael Buckby, Peter Bull, Rob Fletcher, Peter Green, Brian Page and Derek Roger

The number of pupils taking foreign languages has dropped alarmingly over the past few years. This trend could well be reversed, however, by a combination of regular testing and lessons in everyday French, according to this report from the Schools Council Project on Graded Tests in Modern Languages.

Graded syllabuses and tests for foreign languages have been introduced by some schools in about 58 local education authorities throughout the UK over the last five years. However, this has been done on an *ad hoc* basis with little overall evaluation. The present report, undertaken for the Council by the Language Teaching Centre at the University of York in the school year 1978–9, is the first major evaluation of the method. It was found that pupils using graded tests showed significantly more positive attitudes to learning French than control pupils taught by conventional means. This was equally true of pupils of all abilities. Interestingly, while boys are normally less keen on learning French than girls, in the research the experimental boys showed attitudes as positive as those normally held by girls. A key finding was that many more experimental than control pupils chose to carry on with French after options – 62 per cent as against 42 per cent. Sixty-two per cent is about twice the national average.

These research results will boost foreign-language teaching in schools and aid those advocating wider use of graded tests.

Schools Council Publications, 1981. 82pp.
Available from CILT, 20 Carlton House Terrace, London SW1Y 5AP.

Languages other than French in the secondary school
by C. G. Hadley and others

The overwhelming dominance of French in secondary schools can be seen from the proportions of A-level candidates in 1978 – three times as many for French as for German, and 53 times as many as for Russian.

This exploratory study, carried out from 1979 to 1980, investigates the possibility of introducing languages other than French as first foreign language in the secondary school. It describes various strategies for doing this and examines some of the reasons often given against it.

Seventy-five schools offering a non-French language as first or equal first foreign language completed a questionnaire about staffing, period allocation and time-tabling, option schemes, reasons for adopting the language, parental reactions, and so on, and of these twenty-three were selected for detailed study before any questionnaires were despatched and are described fully in this report. The information gained from the answers to the questionnaire gives an insight into the advantages of having a language other than French as first foreign language and the problems involved in introducing it, and the study adumbrates potential fuller reports.

The working party which carried out this exploratory study consisted of members of the Schools Council Modern Languages Committee and representatives of the Joint Council of Language Associations (JCLA), the National Association of Language Advisers (NALA), the National Congress for Languages in Education (NCLE), and the Centre for Information on Language Teaching and Research (CILT).

Schools Council Publications, 1981. 62pp.
Available from CILT, 20 Carlton House Terrace, London SW1Y 5AP.

The practical curriculum

When the Schools Council decided its programme priorities in 1979, having consulted the local authorities, teachers and its other members, it considered that 'there appears to be support for developing a general framework for the curriculum. We propose to engage in discussions about curriculum balance and content. We believe that teachers, schools and local education authorities will welcome a lead from the Council.'

The practical curriculum presents the first fruits of those discussions. It argues that we need to develop a visible structure for the curriculum. A useful starting point is to consider each pupil's right of access to different areas of human knowledge and experience. For each child, what he or she takes away from school is the effective curriculum. This paper emphasizes this different view of the curriculum as the experience each child has at school and what each takes away.

The paper first discusses the principles which underpin a school's curriculum, and then considers the contribution to a child's education made by different kinds of experience and forms of knowledge, modes of teaching and learning, the development of values and attitudes, and the acquisition of skills, including non-verbal skills. Later chapters review the steps involved in planning and monitoring a curriculum and assessing a school's success in meeting its aims.

This contribution to the curriculum debate is addressed first of all to teachers. They are the people who have to resolve the tensions between the delivery of a mass public service open to all children and the individuality of each child. Whatever the outcome of the discussions on freedom and uniformity in the curriculum, many important decisions about what is taught and how it is taught will still be made by schools and by individual teachers. They need a good basis for these decisions, and that is what *The practical curriculum* provides.

Methuen Educational, 1981. 76pp.

Making the most of the short in-service course
by Jean Rudduck

Short in-service courses are the most common form of in-service training, yet there has until recently been little attempt to analyse their potential. Between 1979 and 1980 the Schools Council project, Making the Most of the Short In-Service Course, collaborated with five LEAs in studying local experience of various aspects and styles of in-service courses including short courses that meet once a week for several weeks, a programme of meetings organized by groups of first schools, teacher-tutor schemes, follow-up after a short course is over, and the evaluation of short courses. This report describes several such activities and approaches, draws some general conclusions about effective practice and raises issues for further debate.

Teachers, advisers and teachers' centre wardens alike will find this book invaluable in developing their own in-service courses.

Methuen Educational, 1981. 200pp.

Statistics in schools 11-16: a review
by Peter Holmes, Ramesh Kapadia and G. Neil Rubra, edited by Daphne Turner

This report of the Schools Council Statistical Education Project (11-16), set up at the University of Sheffield in 1975, is a summary of project papers produced by the team in assessing the current situation in statistical education in schools, and covers the use of statistics in many areas of the curriculum.

Chapter I describes a survey carried out by the project team in a 10 per cent sample of all secondary schools in England and Wales. It reveals what statistics is taught, by whom, to whom and in what subjects. Chapter II considers the statistical content of examinations at GCE O and AO levels and in CSE, investigating the incidence of topics and the types of examination questions asked. Chapter III looks more closely at the statistics pupils meet in their mathematics and science lessons, while Chapter IV similarly investigates the use of statistics in humanities and social science courses. In Chapter V the position of probability and statistics in the primary school is considered – providing a useful guide in assessing the statistical background which may be expected of pupils when they start secondary school.

The questionnaire used in the survey is reproduced in the appendices, which also include a review of some standard statistics texts and a comprehensive list of references for in-service courses, equipment, books and articles all relevant to the teaching of statistics.

The report provides useful information on the current position of statistics teaching in schools, and helpful and detailed reviews and lists of resources.

Methuen Educational, 1981. 144pp.

Defining public examination standards
by T. Christie and G. M. Forrest

This report explores the nature of the judgement required when examination boards are charged with responsibility for maintaining standards. Although the argument is generalizable to any public examination structure designed to measure educational achievement, its exposition is confined largely to GCE Advanced-level procedures and in particular to those of the Joint Matriculation Board.

Definitions of standards have stressed the importance of maintaining an equilibrium in examination practice between two types of attainment – either relative to a syllabus or in comparison with the performance of other candidates. JMB current practice is reviewed in order to see how this equilibrium is maintained in grade award meetings; on the basis of an analysis of JMB statistics the authors conclude that the demands of comparability of standards within a subject over time have diverged.

The report considers models of grading, although there appears to be no compelling theoretical reason for adopting any one of the models discussed. The differing benefits of the approaches, emphasizing either parity between subjects or parity between years, are briefly reviewed in the context of four presumed functions of a public examination system, namely the provision of feedback to selectors, pupils, subject teachers and the wider society.

In view of the imminent changes in certification at 16+, and the continuing problems of sixth-form examinations, it is hoped that this study will contribute to agreement on how examination standards should be defined.

Macmillan Education, 1981. 112pp.

Objective assessment by means of item banking
by John Dobby and Derek Duckworth

This bulletin describes work on item banking carried out for the Schools Council by the Examinations and Tests Research Unit of the National Foundation for Educational Research in England and Wales.

The report covers two distinct areas: in Chapters I and II there is a detailed description of an experiment in the use of item banking carried out in conjunction with an examining board and schools in its area, while in Chapters III and IV there is an account of some of the new thinking about item banking which was proceeding in parallel with the empirical investigations.

There is a glossary with definitions and explanations of some of the technical terms used in the bulletin, and included in the appendices are details of a computerized item-banking system which can cope with all the data-handling associated with the creation and use of item banks.

Because of the potential of item banking for overcoming some of the problems of the objective assessment of educational attainment, this bulletin should be of interest to all those involved in this kind of assessment.

Evans/Methuen Educational, 1979. 96pp.

Information skills in the secondary curriculum
edited by Michael Marland

This bulletin has been prepared by a working group sponsored by the British Library and the Schools Council. The recommendations will help middle and secondary schools include in their overall curriculum the development of pupils' information skills: the ability to formulate and focus a question, find possible sources, judge their appropriateness, extract the relevant information, reorganize it and prepare it for future use or presentation to others – in short, to encourage and assist students to organize their learning during school and beyond.

'It is a central responsibility of the school to help its pupils to cope with learning,' state the authors, and '... information skills can only be satisfactorily incorporated in the school's programme by a curriculum policy built around these skills'. The working group, by dissecting an apparently simple assignment, identifies a series of stages, nine 'question steps', which students need to work through. These stages are examined, and ways in which teachers might stimulate the development of the necessary study skills are discussed, together with their relationship to the overall curriculum.

Every teacher will be interested in this report because the general principles apply to learning tasks given to pupils and students of all ages.

Methuen Educational, 1981. 64pp.